ALL DAY
VEGAN

ALL DAY
VEGAN

100 PLANT-BASED RECIPES TO ENJOY ANY TIME OF DAY

MINA ROME

Publisher Mike Sanders
Art & Design Director William Thomas
Editor Brandon Buechley
Designer Lindsay Dobbs
Illustrator Artemis Chodzinski
Proofreader Megan Douglass
Indexer Johnna VanHoose Dinse

First American Edition, 2022
Published in the United States by DK Publishing
1745 Broadway, 20th Floor, New York, NY 10019

A catalog record for this book
is available from the Library of Congress.
ISBN 978-0-7440-5494-1

DK books are available at special discounts when purchased
in bulk for sales promotions, premiums, fund-raising, or
educational use. For details, contact: DK Publishing Special
Markets,
1745 Broadway, 20th Floor, New York, NY 10019
SpecialSales@dk.com

Printed and bound in China

Photography © Amina Romdhani
Illustrations © Artemis Chodzinski

For the curious
www.dk.com

ABOUT MINA

Mina is an author and the creator of the YouTube channel *Mina Rome*. With her quick and easy recipes, detailed camerawork, and focus on plant-based ingredients, Mina has captured the attention of many. Her recipes cover all aspects of vegan cooking, offering ideas and variations along the way so anyone—regardless of experience cooking vegan dishes—can find something to enjoy.

ACKNOWLEDGMENTS

First, I'd like to thank Artemis, without whom this book would have turned out only half as beautiful.

And a huge thank you to Nina, for supporting me emotionally during all those late-night photo shoots.

To my family, for happily taste testing each and every recipe.

To my editor, Brandon, for doing an amazing job at making my words make sense.

To my designer, Lindsay, for building the most beautiful book with my words and photos.

And to everybody else who lent me their hands for this project. Seriously, thanks for hand modeling, you guys.

CONTENTS

HELLO THERE!

Welcome to ... my book? This feels surreal to say—or to write, rather—as I usually introduce people to little food videos on my YouTube channel this way.

For quite a few years now, I've been sharing my vegan recipes with people on the internet. Most times, my videos revolve around simple and easy meals you can put together in a pinch. Other times, they feature me taking a stab at more elaborate recipe endeavors, such as baking Zodiac-themed birthday cakes, or re-creating meals from popular vampire romance novels.

With my content, whether it's online or here in this book, I simply want to showcase how fun, delicious, unique, and beautiful vegan food can be.

I love to cook, believe it or not! Making food for myself is absolute self-care. It sounds cliché, but cooking is almost meditative for me. It gives me the opportunity to occupy my mind with simple steps, staying in the moment, rather than worrying about anything else I can't control. And I think cooking with others is even better. It's my favorite way of spending time with family and friends, so I recommend getting together with some of your loved ones to test out the dishes in this book. After all, there are more than 100 recipes to choose from in these pages (don't ask me which is my favorite—I love them all!), so I am certain you'll find something for everyone to enjoy!

Happy cooking!

Mina ♡

INTRODUCTION

"VEGAN FOOD IS BORING"

Of all the negative assumptions one might make about the vegan diet, thinking it is boring hurts my heart the most. I mean, sure, plain rice and beans with a side of trail mix and celery juice doesn't sound very appealing to me either, but trust me, it doesn't have to be this way. I've been working with nothing but vegan food for the past seven years, and it's been a tasty seven years, I have to say.

Removing animal products from my diet seemed at first like an insurmountable restriction, but it soon opened my mind and expanded my food and cooking horizons so much more.

I was introduced to so many plant-based ingredients I'd never heard of before, and had no choice but to figure out how to get as much flavor as possible out of these new, mysterious foods. And thus you could definitely say that, through lots of trial and error, I became a much better cook as a result. And it became especially fun for me—creating my own dishes and sharing them with my (sometimes pretty skeptical) family members. Honestly, nothing is more gratifying to me than seeing a picky eater enjoy something I have made.

Vegan cooking is not about accurately replicating animal product dishes, such as an actual steak (although this can make for a fun challenge, and my **Maple Mustard–Glazed Seitan Steaks** are definitely worth a try), but about creating delicious meals that can stand on their own two flavorful feet—dishes that taste amazing and just so happen to be plant-based.

There are about a hundred recipes in this book alone that prove just how good vegan food can be. These recipes occasionally reference traditionally non-vegan meals in the title (**Basil "Ricotta" Pasta**, for example), but their flavors are, although varied and unique, just as yummy and satisfying as the original.

Plant-based food is so incredibly versatile. It can be hearty and satisfying (**One Pot Hummus Ramen** or **Rice Paper Tteokbokki Soup**) or light and fresh (**Everything Bagel & Kale Summer Rolls** or **Banh Mi–Style Salad**). You can make meals that are super quick and simple (**Lemon Tofu** or **Chickpea Pancakes**) or a little more impressive or fancy/chic (**Potato & Thyme Galette** or the **Enchilada Crunch Wraps**) (I'm pretty sure nobody has called a crunch wrap fancy or chic before, but, trust me, you'll feel like a pro chef serving these).

Everyday vegan meals can easily go beyond your classic banana bread, avocado toast, and falafel with hummus rotation. These are all delicious things to start with, but creating recipes gets really fun when you draw inspiration from simpler or standard meals and use them in a creative new way! And just like that, you have recipes for **Peanut Butter Banana Bread Granola, Overnight Tofu Avocado Toast,** and **Falafel Crumble Tacos.**

On top of that, pretty much every recipe in this book includes ideas for ingredient alterations. This allows for even more variations, giving you countless ways of enjoying each of these vegan recipes.

You really don't have to compromise flavor when choosing to cook vegan. Whether you simply want to eat less meat or include more fruits and vegetables in your diet, or you're already living the full-on plant-based lifestyle and are in desperate need of some new ideas, *All Day Vegan* has you covered!

HOW TO USE THIS BOOK

This book is going to walk you through an entire day of eating. The recipes are divided into five categories: Breakfast, Lunch, Snacks, Dinner, and Dessert. I cover as much ground as I can with these recipes, designing them in a way that makes them fit into all types of daily situations: a quick and easy breakfast for you and your roommate; a birthday cake you want to bake for your best friend; an easy, yet fancy, date night dinner; a single serving dessert to treat yourself with after a long day at work; and so on. Of course, you can easily scale these recipes up or down to make them work best for you. And you don't have to be a home chef to get started on any of these, as I'll be here with you every step of the way!

Each recipe includes most of the following: a list of ingredients, a breakdown of the steps, a rough indicator of cooking and preparation times (cooking time meaning the time your food will spend bubbling away on the stove or sitting in the oven, and preparation time reflecting the time you'll be spending chopping, kneading, rolling, etc.), an estimate of how many servings you'll be left with in the end (keep in mind serving sizes vary from person to person), useful tips and notes to aid you in the experience, and a photo of the finished dish, along with any necessary step-by-step photos to guide you through the more complex recipe directions.

GET CREATIVE

While *All Day Vegan* is said to include 100 recipes, it actually has so much more to offer. Whether it be suggestions on spices, toppings, or sides of choice, or ideas on how to pair different recipes in the book together, *All Day Vegan* offers the tools you need to create the best plant-based meals for any taste buds on any occasion imaginable.

This book is all about fostering creativity within a seemingly limited field of options. You are not as limited as you think, whether that be with plant-based ingredients, or the ideas I offer up in this book. I encourage you to think outside the box and have fun with these recipes! Sure, experimentation can sometimes yield some less-than-desirable results, but with my guidance and your creativity, I'm certain we can cook up some amazing dishes!

GOING GLOBAL

I am from Germany—land of punctuality, great whole wheat bread, and amazing vegan substitute products. In this book, you'll find standard plant-based products being used, such as vegan milk, butter, cream, cream cheese, and much more. However, I'm aware these ingredients may vary depending on where in the world you are. While I believe most of these items should be fairly accessible to many, a little extra research can go a long way in ensuring you're working with the right tools. My hope is that the variations I provide for many of the recipes in this book will allow you to enjoy the end result, no matter where you live or what your local stores provide.

DELICIOUS VISUALS

If you're a visual person like me, I want to take a moment to get you hyped for the artwork in this cookbook. It's so fun! I love creating recipe videos because they allow me to get creative with how I visually display my recipes. Knowing that, for a book, I would only have photos to work with had me feeling incredibly intimidated at first. I knew I wouldn't be able to hide behind musical edits and clever, fast-paced cuts. Everything had to be captured in just a single frame. It was a lot of work but I am just so happy with how everything came together!

You'll also notice the beautiful food illustrations created by my dear friend, Artemis. I am just so in love with her adorable, cartoonish versions of the food in this book! Collaborating with her on my cookbook was honestly a dream come true.

EQUIPMENT

Before we get cooking, let's have a look at what you'll need in your kitchen to get started.

DIGITAL SCALE & MEASURING CUPS

How do we best measure our ingredients? Personally, I like to use both the metric system and the cup system. For recipes where accuracy isn't super important, I tend to go with cups. These measure ingredients based on volume, which isn't always the most precise. Using a digital kitchen scale is the best way to get the most accurate measurement. Use one that allows you to weigh liquids as well. Mine can differentiate between weighing oils, water, and milk, which is incredibly practical. That being said, cups will not give you a drastically different result, so use the method that works for you.

TABLESPOONS (TBSP) & TEASPOONS (TSP)

Many people use measuring spoon sets where a tablespoon yields around 10 to 15 milliliters and a teaspoon around 5 milliliters. However, I find that using such a set can be a bit tedious at times, so I typically just go for solo tablespoons and teaspoons. When it comes to measuring smaller amounts, such as ½ teaspoon, I simply eyeball it, although less so when baking.

BOWLS

It's useful to have a variety of small, medium, and large bowls in the kitchen.

CUTTING BOARDS

Whether it be for chopping vegetables or kneading dough, you'll find yourself working with cutting boards more often than you'd expect.

KNIVES

Small knives that are sharp and feel good in your hands are perfect here. Always be careful and stay focused when cutting anything. Don't chop a zucchini while watching reality TV, for example. No, I'm not speaking from experience. Why do you ask?

POTS, PANS & SKILLETS

Small, medium, and large non-stick skillets are my go-tos, but, for some recipes, stainless steel or heavy cast-iron skillets work even better. These distribute the heat more evenly than non-stick, and therefore allow for crispier foods. However, foods have a higher risk of sticking to them.

While not essential, grill pans, which give your foods that nice barbecue-stripe look, are also nice to have.

SIEVES & STRAINERS

Fine mesh or metal strainers are the most handy since you can use them for draining and rinsing pasta, beans, rice, and much more. I would recommend one small, one medium, and one large metal mesh sieve. The small ones are perfect for dusting powdered sugar or cocoa powder over your dishes!

WHISKS, WOODEN SPOONS, & SPATULAS

Cooking spatulas are great for flipping things and pressing them into your pan. My favorite is a heat-resistant plastic spatula. This won't scratch your pan like a metal one might.

Baking spatulas, usually made of silicone, are wonderful for scraping cake batter out of a bowl, frosting cakes, or simply mixing things. These two spatulas are similar, but their uses are totally different.

BLENDER

A high speed blender is really useful. But don't worry, it doesn't need to cost the same amount as a car. Affordable, high-quality options are out there. I recommend using a blender that holds up to 6 cups (1,500ml) with a fitting tamper stick.

FOOD PROCESSOR

I recommend using a food processor that holds up to 5 cups (1,250ml). Keep in mind that larger food processors will have a more difficult time blending smaller volumes.

ELECTRIC HAND MIXER

While not essential, an electric hand mixer is great to have. A whisk and some extra muscle power can get the same job done!

BAKING PANS

Baking pans are essential for any baker. This book requires a 12 cup muffin pan, an 8-inch (20cm) square brownie pan, an 8-inch (20cm) round springform pan, an 8-inch (20cm) loaf pan, a 10-inch (25cm) loaf pan, a 10-inch (25cm) springform pan, and 4 6 to 8 ounce (180ml to 240ml) ramekins.

However, I don't want you to feel the need to go out and buy all of these at once! If you're just getting started building your collection of baking equipment, start slow and purchase them when you really need them. When baking on a budget, ask family and friends if you can borrow theirs.

BAKING BRUSHES

Baking brushes are perfect for oiling baking pans or gently brushing liquids onto foods.

ICE CREAM SCOOPS

Ice cream scoops are not essential, but I love them! I use mine for much more than just ice cream. It's perfect for portioning equal amounts of cookie dough, muffin batter, or pancake batter in a clean fashion. Make sure there is a lever to dispense each scoop.

INGREDIENTS

Here is a list of ingredients you'll see pop up the most throughout the recipes in this book.

APPLESAUCE (UNSWEETENED)
This is a wonderful, relatively flavor-neutral egg substitute used in vegan baking.

BAKING POWDER
This is very important, as vegan baking needs all the rising agent it can get.

BEANS
These make for an incredible source of protein. My favorites are chickpeas and edamame.

BITTERSWEET CHOCOLATE
Many of my recipes use this chocolate. Make sure it's vegan. Most bittersweet chocolate in Europe is naturally vegan.

COCOA POWDER (UNSWEETENED)
This gives your food a deep chocolatey flavor. Different brands may vary in intensity and bitterness. Do not confuse this with cocoa mix, which oftentimes comes with added sugars and milk powder.

CORNSTARCH
This is a perfect thickening agent for sauces and custards. The starch always needs to be fully mixed into cold liquid before boiling, otherwise it may clump up. Once the starch reaches boiling point, it thickens. Always mix vigorously and continuously when cooking with cornstarch.

DATES
These are natural sweeteners and, in combination with salted nut butter, one of the best snacks of all time. In all my recipes I use Deglet Noor dates, which have a milder sweetness compared to other types of dates.

FLAX SEEDS (GROUND)
These are a great source of omega 3, oftentimes used as a thickening or binding agent. Always buy ground or semi-ground flax seeds, as opposed to whole. The ground seeds are much easier to digest.

FLAX MEAL
This is a fine powder that forms as a by-product during flax oil production. It has pretty much the same effect as ground flax seeds, but, in my experience, it draws in more liquid.

FLOUR
I tend to bake with all-purpose or white spelt flour. For my Germans, all-purpose refers to flours type 405 and 550.

FRUITS AND VEGETABLES
Go get those daily vitamins!

GARLIC
Yes, this is a vegetable, but it's an important flavor booster and therefore gets its own moment to shine on this list. Garlic burns super fast, so always make sure to cook it on low to medium heat.

GRAINS

There are so many great grains out there: millet, couscous, quinoa, rice, and more. Choose what works best for you.

GREENS

Yes, this is also technically vegetables. Fresh baby spinach is my preferred green to use.

HERBS

Whether fresh, frozen, or dried, these are perfect for adding freshness to your dishes.

HUMMUS

I go through a tub of plain store-bought hummus every week, it seems. I use it in so many things: sandwiches, pasta sauces, dips, soups, dressings, and more.

KALA NAMAK

Also known as black salt, this ingredient adds the flavor of eggs to your meals. Sprinkle it over right before serving for that fully authentic sulfurous flavor.

LENTILS

These are a great source of protein. My go-tos are canned brown lentils and beluga.

LEMON (LIME) JUICE

I love tanginess in my food, which is why I often add a drizzle of citrus over my meals. This is also perfect for replacing apple cider vinegar when baking, or white wine vinegar in savory recipes.

LIQUID SWEETENER

Maple syrup, agave syrup, rice syrup, and date syrup, among others, all come with slightly different levels of sweetness, but are still relatively interchangeable. I especially love maple syrup for its naturally sweet caramel flavor.

MISO PASTE

Otherwise known as fermented soybean paste, this is a very salty and very flavorful ingredient. A little goes a long way!

NON-DAIRY MILK

The world of plant milks is very diverse these days. Classic oat and soy remain my personal favorites, but you can find a wide variety to choose from.

NUT BUTTER

If it were humanly possible to only consume peanut butter for the rest of my life, I would gladly do so. I'm talking natural peanut butter, consisting only of peanuts and salt. Almond and cashew butter are other favorites of mine.

NUTRITIONAL YEAST

This is deactivated yeast used to give your food a savory, almost cheese-like flavor.

NUTS

These are a wonderful source of healthy fats and protein.

OATS

I love baking with oats! I use quick-cooking oats the most. Sometimes, I also go for old fashioned or rolled oats. Oat flour is created by simply chopping up oats in a food processor until fine.

OIL

Olive, sunflower, and coconut oils are my preferred choices. When I refer to vegetable oil in a recipe, feel free to use your preferred oil of the bunch, or what works for you.

ONION

Whether yellow, white, red, or green onion, a quick onion sauté is how many recipes begin. Green onion is great for sprinkling over your finished dish!

RICE PAPER

One of the cleverest food inventions of all time, these translucent sheets become malleable when dipped into water for a few seconds. You can turn rice paper into rice cakes or summer rolls, or bake them all crispy to make a bacon substitute.

SEEDS

Sunflower, hemp, and sesame are my go-tos. I tend to sprinkle sesame seeds over everything. They are pretty and good for you!

SALT

Obviously vital in cooking, but underrated when it comes to baking sweet food, you'll find salt in nearly every recipe.

SPICES

You are always encouraged to season your food as much as you want, with whatever you want. I'm here to merely give you suggestions and ideas.

SPICY CONDIMENTS

Only you know your spice tolerance, but I love adding sriracha, harissa, and gochujang to my dishes occasionally.

SUGAR

I typically use regular white sugar, but sometimes I also go for brown, raw cane, or coconut sugar when it suits the recipe.

TAHINI

Otherwise known as blended sesame seed paste. In my recipes, I'm always referring to white tahini, made out of 100% hulled sesame seeds. If you can't find this, you should be good using regular brown tahini, just keep in mind that it's a bit more bitter.

TAPIOCA STARCH

This is a thickening agent that, when heated up, gives liquids a stringy and almost melted cheese-like consistency, which is why it's the main ingredient in my **Ultimate Vegan Grilled Cheese (page 78)**. Keep in mind that tapioca starch and cornstarch are not interchangeable.

TEMPEH

This is a great source of protein made from fermented soy beans. Tempeh does have a subtle bitter taste some people may not enjoy. To alleviate this bitterness, simply boil or steam the tempeh pieces for 15 to 20 minutes before marinating. I often skip this process, as the natural tempeh flavor doesn't bother me.

TOFU

Tofu can have a reputation for being boring, but I beg to differ. It is one of the most versatile products out there, and due to its mild natural flavor, it can take on any new flavor you give it.

TORTILLAS

I love using these! My book calls for small, medium, and large flour or corn tortillas.

VANILLA

Many of my recipes call for vanilla. Vanilla extract, sugar, or baking aroma all get the job done, depending on the recipe.

VEGAN BUTTER

Vegan butter or margarine will show up in many of my recipes, especially the baking ones.

VEGAN DAIRY

Think yogurt, cream cheese, sour cream, and cheese—all made from plants. Depending on where you're at in the world, you might have access to different products than I do. Definitely test out these products first and find your favorites before getting started with these recipes!

VINEGAR

Acidic components are so important when cooking. Vegan white wine vinegar has a nice and mild tangy flavor, which is why I use it in almost all my recipes. I tend to use apple cider vinegar when baking. When preparing a dressing, I often choose rice vinegar.

VITAL WHEAT GLUTEN

This is a fine powder consisting of pure gluten. It can be used to make seitan or be added to flour to give your baked goods a more elastic, chewy texture.

THE MORE YOU KNOW

Together with my community I've compiled this list of quick and helpful cooking and baking tips!

BUILD A SOLID BASE

Every recipe seems to start with a quick onion and garlic sauté, right? Sometimes, spices are added; sometimes there are other vegetables involved like carrots, peppers, ginger, etc. This simple first step of sautéeing finely chopped vegetables in oil is super important, as it gives your entire dish a deeper flavor profile. You can create endless versions of these base mixtures: use vegetables you're unfamiliar with; switch up the use of fat; cook your vegetables longer than usual, but on low heat; add some dried herbs; or experiment with spices. Have fun!

UMAMI UMAMI UMAMI

This is the savory, hearty, "meaty" flavor component to a dish. It may not seem so, but there are plenty of plant based sources of umami out there. Some examples include miso paste, seaweed, smoked tofu, soy sauce, vegan Worcestershire sauce, nutritional yeast, mushrooms, tomato paste, olives, and capers, among others. Add these to your recipes! The umami factor can also be boosted by; sautéeing or grilling vegetables (see above); cooking or deglazing your vegetables with a splash of an alcoholic drink such as wine or beer; adding spices like smoked paprika powder, curry powder, garlic, or onion powder; and adding premade sauces and condiments such as vegan barbecue sauce, hummus, or vegan mayonnaise.

BALANCE THE SWEET AND SOUR

The sweet and sour flavors are often overlooked when seasoning savory foods. Getting the two of them into balance can take your cooking up to a whole new level. For example, you can do that by adding just 1 teaspoon of maple syrup to your tomato sauce or adding 1 tablespoon of lemon juice to your pumpkin soup.

ADD SALT TO SWEET

This is also an underrated combo. Adding a tiny bit of salt while cooking or baking something sweet is an absolute game changer. Have you ever dipped salted pretzels in chocolate hazelnut spread? Or added a pinch of salt to your oatmeal? As a child, I would dip my fries in vanilla milkshakes. While maybe a little extreme, I clearly understood the concept.

SEASON TO TASTE ALONG THE WAY

Instead of seasoning the finished meal, season every layer and portion of your dish. For instance, add some spices to your vegetable sauté, some spices and salt to your sauce, and don't forget the salt in your pasta water! In general, always season according to your taste buds. Go with your gut, literally! But keep in mind that with some ingredients, you don't want to be adding salt in the beginning of the process. For example, lentils need to cook through before salt is added, or they'll stay tough.

SLOW & LOW IS BETTER THAN QUICK & HIGH

For the first few years cooking for myself, I would usually sauté quickly on high heat and burn half my food. Only later did I realize how much of a difference it makes to give your ingredients a little extra time, keeping them on medium or even medium-low to low heat. This ensures your ingredients release all of their delicious flavors and, as an added bonus, you won't accidentally be scorching your dinner!

USE WHAT YOU HAVE AND GET CREATIVE

Using what you have and getting creative is hands down the best form of home cooking practice there is. Trying and failing and learning along the way about what to do and what not to do is going to make you become a confident home chef. Plus, it's more sustainable to use what you have first, rather than running out and grabbing shiny new things from the store.

HERBS HERBS HERBS

Sometimes, all your meal needs is a little extra freshness in the form of herbs! Basil, dill, parsley, cilantro—you name it!

DON'T UNDERESTIMATE TOPPINGS

Fun toppings can really save any dish; not just visually, but also in flavor. Adding some fresh green onion, roasted sesame seeds, an additional squeeze of lime, a drizzle of hot sauce, a sprinkle of nutritional yeast, or a spoonful of vegan cream cheese can help your dish go from just okay to pretty amazing!

WET THE PARCHMENT PAPER

You might see this tip pop up a few times in the recipes in this book. Wetting parchment paper makes it more malleable and, therefore, it aligns better with the shape of the baking dish. Simply hold the paper under running water for a few short seconds. It shouldn't be dripping wet, but just moist enough for you to easily crumble it into a ball. Unfold the ball and you have a sheet of parchment that's much easier to work with.

BOIL THE CASHEWS

Cashews are often puréed to give foods a rich and creamy texture. This is perfect for pasta sauces, dips, or frostings. In order for the nuts to blend nicely, you can either let them soak in water 8 hours prior to blending, or you can boil them in water for 20 to 25 minutes. I prefer the latter much more. The boiling gives the cashews a richer flavor. I find that blending boiled nuts always comes out smoother than blending soaked nuts.

REVIVE THOSE DATES

Here is another one you'll find often in these pages. If your dates seem a little too dry to blend, whether for smoothies, energy bites, or frostings, simply let them soak in a bowl of hot water for 10 to 15 minutes to hydrate.

CLEAN UP AS YOU COOK

I still need to be reminded of this obvious tip once in a while. Being an adult is hard, but you gotta do what you gotta do! Tidy up a little as you're waiting on some foods to finish cooking. Putting away the last few things as you're waiting for your food to cool down allows for maximum efficiency.

TOMATO PASTE VS TOMATO PUREE

What many call tomato purée, those in the U.S. call tomato paste. You'll find this dynamically named ingredient often in this book, so I urge you to identify the correct name for this tomato product in your location before you start cooking.

HAVE FUN

This is arguably the most important tip of all! Put on some good tunes or a fun podcast. Cook with a buddy. Make it an event. Enjoy the process! The food always seems to taste better this way.

BREAKFAST

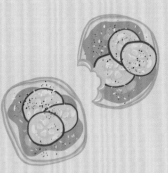

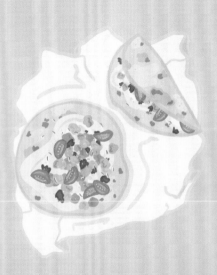

CHOCOLATE POLENTA PORRIDGE

PREP TIME: 6 MINUTES
COOK TIME: 10 MINUTES
YIELD: 1 SERVING

INGREDIENTS

1¼ cup (310ml) nondairy
   milk, plus more for serving

½ tsp vanilla extract

1 tbsp maple syrup

pinch of salt

1¼ tbsp unsweetened cocoa
   powder

⅓ cup (55g) dry polenta

1 tbsp vegan protein powder
   (optional)

1 to 2 tbsp vegan dark
   chocolate chips

Do you ever get bored of basic oatmeal? Try this rich and chocolatey polenta porridge instead!

1 In a small saucepan on medium heat, bring the milk, vanilla, and syrup to a simmer.

2 Meanwhile, in a bowl, combine the salt, cocoa powder, polenta, and the protein powder, if using.

3 Add the combined dry ingredients to the simmering milk, whisking throughout. Let the mixture cook on medium for 2 to 3 minutes, or until nicely thickened. Be sure to stir frequently.

4 Cover the pot with a lid and remove from the heat. Allow the porridge to sit and steam for 3 to 5 minutes, or until the polenta is fully soft.

5 Serve topped with dark chocolate chips and an additional splash of nondairy milk.

BURRITO-STYLE OATS

PREP TIME: 10 MINUTES
COOK TIME: 12 MINUTES
YIELD: 1 SERVING

INGREDIENTS

for the porridge base:

½ cup (45g) quick-cooking
   oats

1 tbsp nutritional yeast

1 to 2 tsp ground flax seeds

dash of ground cumin

dash of paprika

dash of ground pepper

pinch of chili flakes

¼ tsp salt, or to taste

1 cup (250ml) vegetable
   broth

juice of ½ lime

for the black bean topping:

⅓ cup (60g) black beans,
   rinsed and drained

1 tsp ketchup

½ tsp sriracha or similar hot
   sauce, or to taste

serving options:

tortilla chips, store bought
   or homemade (recipe on
   page 118)

vegan sour cream

avocado

diced tomatoes

salsa

fresh parsley or cilantro

hemp, sunflower, or sesame
   seeds

Savory porridge may sound strange, but trust me, it works! This is my take on the breakfast burrito, you could say.

1 In a small saucepan, combine the oats, yeast, flax seeds, cumin, paprika, black pepper, chili flakes, salt, vegetable broth, and lime juice. Bring to a boil on high heat, then reduce to medium. Let this cook for 6 to 8 minutes, or until you reach the desired consistency. Make sure to stir frequently. If the mixture becomes too thick, add a splash of water.

2 Meanwhile, in a separate small saucepan, heat the black beans, ketchup, sriracha, and a splash of water for 2 to 3 minutes on medium-high. Alternatively, heat for 1 minute on high in the microwave. Mash the beans with a fork.

3 Add the oat mixture to a bowl and top with the beans and any of the serving options listed. Enjoy!

CHERRY CHEESECAKE BAKED OATS

PREP TIME: 5 MINUTES
COOK TIME: 30 MINUTES
YIELD: 2 SERVINGS

INGREDIENTS

vegetable oil, for greasing

1 cup (90g) quick-cooking oats

1 tbsp ground flax seeds

⅓ tsp salt

1 tsp baking powder

¾ cup (97g) pitted frozen cherries, divided

1 tsp vanilla extract

¼ cup (60ml) nondairy milk

2 tsp apple cider vinegar

3 tbsp applesauce

2½ tbsp agave or maple syrup

1½ tbsp sunflower seed oil

2 tbsp vegan cream cheese or thick soy yogurt, divided

2 vegan cookies or graham crackers, crushed (optional)

Treat yourself to these fancy little oat cakes! They're cherry-filled with a cream cheese center and a cookie topping. What's not to like?

1   Lightly oil two 6 or 8 oz (180 or 240ml) ramekins or bowls of similar size. If using the oven, preheat to 350°F (180°C).

2   In a blender, add the oats, flax seeds, salt, baking powder, ½ cup (65g) frozen cherries, vanilla, milk, vinegar, applesauce, syrup, and sunflower seed oil. Blend until smooth.

3   Add the remaining ¼ cup (32g) of cherries to the blender and pulse a few seconds so the cherry chunks are distributed evenly without being fully blended.

4   Divide the batter evenly between the two ramekins.

5   Add 1 tablespoon of vegan cream cheese to the center of each bowl, pushing it down under the surface of the batter. Bake for 30 minutes or microwave on high for 4 to 5 minutes, checking up on it every 30 seconds.

6   Let cool for at least 15 minutes before serving. If desired, crumble the cookies or graham crackers over the top.

Tip: In order for your cheesecakes to turn out as red as mine, add a few drops of plant-based red food coloring to the blended mixture in step 2.

LEMON PIE OATMEAL

PREP TIME: 12 MIN
COOK TIME: 15 MIN
YIELD: 1 SERVING

INGREDIENTS

for the lemon curd:

⅓ cup (80ml) nondairy milk

3 tbsp sugar

¼ tsp salt

2 tbsp vegan butter

zest of 1 lemon

¼ cup (60ml) fresh lemon
  juice (about 2 lemons)

2 tsp cornstarch

2 tbsp water

a few drops of plant-based
  yellow food coloring
  (optional)

for the oatmeal:

½ cup (45g) quick-cooking
  oats

pinch of salt

2 tsp ground flax seeds

1 cup (250ml) nondairy milk

for serving:

a few tbsp thick soy yogurt

1 to 2 tbsp almond slivers

I love dessert-inspired breakfast. Here we have a bowl of classic porridge topped with yogurt, toasted almond slivers, and homemade lemon curd.

1 To prepare the lemon curd, add the milk, sugar, salt, butter, lemon zest, and lemon juice to a small saucepan. In a small glass or bowl, combine the cornstarch and water until no clumps remain. Add this to the saucepan. Bring to a boil on high heat, stirring frequently. Reduce heat to medium and let simmer for about 2 minutes or until thickened. The sauce should still be nice and pourable. Lastly, stir in a few drops of food coloring, if desired. Transfer the curd to a small jar. This sauce yields enough for 4 to 5 servings of oats. Keep stored in the fridge for up to one week. Consider making this the night before to save time.

2 Place the oats, salt, flax seeds, and milk in a small saucepan. Stir well.

3 Bring the mixture to a boil on high heat, then reduce the heat to medium and let simmer, stirring frequently, for about 5 minutes, or until the desired consistency has been achieved. If the mixture becomes too thick, add an additional splash of milk.

4 Heat a small skillet on medium-high. Add the almond slivers. Toast the nuts for about 2 minutes until golden brown, stirring occasionally.

5 Assemble! Serve your oats with a few teaspoons of thick vegan yogurt, the toasted nuts, and a few teaspoons of lemon curd drizzled over top. Be sure to stir the curd before adding it to the oats. Enjoy!

Tip: I highly recommend saving some of this curd to use as a pancake topping. You can find my pancake recipe on **page 46**.

CHAI TOAST CRUNCH

This crunchy, chai-spiced cereal is perfect for preparing in advance. Perhaps on a cozy Sunday night? This way, you can snack on it throughout the week!

PREP TIME: 40 MIN (PLUS RESTING TIME)
COOK TIME: 20 MIN
YIELD: 6 TO 8 SERVINGS

INGREDIENTS

1 tbsp flax meal

3 tbsp water

½ cup (113g) vegan butter, softened

1 tsp vanilla extract

⅓ cup plus 1 tbsp (75g) coconut sugar or sugar

2 tbsp maple or brown rice syrup

1½ cup plus 2 tbsp (200g) all-purpose flour (plus more for surface and rolling pin)

½ cup (60g) whole wheat flour

½ tsp baking powder

1 tsp ground cinnamon

½ tsp ground ginger

½ tsp ground cardamom

¼ tsp ground cloves

¼ tsp ground nutmeg

¼ tsp ground black pepper

¼ tsp salt

optional:

2 tbsp melted vegan butter, divided

2 tbsp sugar plus ½ tsp ground cinnamon (combine to make cinnamon sugar), divided

1   In a small bowl, combine the flax meal and water to create a thick flax paste. Set aside.

2   In a large bowl, add the softened butter, vanilla, and sugar. Using an electric hand mixer, beat together for 1 to 2 minutes, or until light and fluffy.

3   Add the flax paste and syrup to the butter mixture. Mix with the hand mixer until combined. Add the all-purpose flour, whole wheat flour, baking powder, spices, and salt. Mix until a dough forms.

4   Transfer the dough to a lightly floured surface and, using your hands, shape it into a big ball. Wrap it up in parchment paper and leave it in the fridge for at least 2 hours, but not more than 3 days.

5   Now onto shaping the cereal! First, preheat the oven to 350°F (180°C) and line two baking sheets with parchment paper.

6   Cut the chilled dough in half and place one half back into the fridge. You will be working with one half at a time.

7   Shape the cereal in one of two styles (see photo 1).

    Ball: For each piece of cereal, take a small, hazelnut-size amount of dough and roll it into a little ball. Place it on the lined baking sheet. Continue with as many as will fit onto the baking sheets, while still having about 1 centimeter of space between each one.

    Square: On a generously floured cutting surface, and using a floured rolling pin, roll out the dough until it has reached about half a centimeter in thickness. Trim the edges so you have a large, clean looking rectangle. The scraps can be rerolled together with the second batch. Cut the sheet of dough into small squares (1.5x1.5 cm at most) and transfer them to the prepared baking sheets.

8   **Optional Step:** Brush the tops of the unbaked cereal with 1 tablespoon of melted vegan butter and sprinkle with 1 tablespoon of cinnamon sugar before baking (see photo 2).

9   Bake the squares for 8 to 10 minutes, or until golden brown along the edges.

10 As the first batch is baking, repeat steps 7 and 8 with the remaining half of dough. If there is dough left over after batch two, make a third.

11 Let the cereal cool down fully. Then serve! Enjoy with some cold nondairy milk or use as a topping for future smoothie bowls. Store the remaining cereal in an airtight container for up to two weeks.

1

2

PEANUT BUTTER BANANA BREAD GRANOLA

PREP TIME: 12 MINUTES
COOK TIME: 35 MINUTES
YIELD: 6 TO 8 SERVINGS

INGREDIENTS

1 medium banana, mashed

¼ cup (62g) peanut butter

2½ tbsp solid coconut oil or vegan butter

¼ cup (60ml) maple syrup

2 tbsp brown sugar or coconut sugar

1½ cups (135g) quick-cooking oats

1 cup (90g) old-fashioned oats

⅓ cup (45g) peanuts

2 tbsp hemp, ground flax, or chia seeds

⅓ cup (40g) whole wheat flour

½ tsp salt

½ tsp ground cinnamon

1 tbsp nondairy milk, if needed

A food combination you can never go wrong with. This granola is incredibly crunchy, and a great addition to every bowl of museli.

1 Preheat the oven to 325°F (170°C) and line a baking sheet with parchment paper.

2 In a small saucepan on medium heat, add the mashed banana, peanut butter, coconut oil, syrup, and sugar, stirring thoroughly. Remove from heat once everything has melted together.

3 In a large bowl, combine the quick-cooking oats, old-fashioned oats, peanuts, seeds, flour, salt, and cinnamon. Add the contents from the saucepan. Mix well. If the mixture feels too dry, add 1 tablespoon of nondairy milk.

4 Transfer the mixture to the baking sheet. Spread it flat across the baking sheet and bake for 20 minutes.

5 Leaving the granola on the baking sheet (and being careful not to burn yourself!), immediately cut into about 20 pieces of equal size. A butter knife should do the trick. Bake for an additional 8 to 10 minutes.

6 The pieces in the center of the tray may need some extra time in the oven. If so, remove the golden brown pieces along the edges and set them aside. Give the remaining granola another 5 to 7 minutes of baking time and then let cool.

7 Once cool, break the granola apart into bite-size pieces and store in an airtight container. I recommend serving with some **Peanut Milk (page 144)**!

Tip: Feel free to add some vegan chocolate chips or cranberries to your cooled granola for some extra flavor.

GOOD MORNING MATE SMOOTHIE

PREP TIME: 5 MINUTES (PLUS
    OVERNIGHT TEA STEEP)
COOK TIME: NONE
YIELD: 1 SERVING

INGREDIENTS

3 to 4 dates, pitted

1 yerba mate, black, or chai
    tea bag

¾ cup (180ml) hot water,
    more if needed

½ tsp lemon zest

2 tbsp lemon juice

1 to 2 frozen bananas,
    chopped

1 tbsp nut butter (cashew
    butter preferred)

2 tsp ground flax seeds

This overnight tea smoothie using yerba mate will wake you up quickly! I often look forward to its lemon cake batter taste in the morning.

1   The night before, add the dates and tea bag to a small pot. Pour the hot water over and cover. If using mate or black tea, let it steep for around 5 minutes before removing the bag. If using chai tea, leave the bag to steep overnight. Also let the dates soak in the tea overnight.

2   The next morning, add the dates, tea, lemon zest, lemon juice, bananas, nut butter, and flax seeds to a blender and blend until smooth. Serve immediately.

Tip: Frozen apples are a great substitute for bananas in this recipe. Cut them into slices before freezing. Peeling them is optional.

CHOCOLATE ZUCCHINI SHAKE

PREP TIME: 5 MINUTES (PLUS
   FREEZING TIME)
COOK TIME: NONE
YIELD: 1 SERVING

INGREDIENTS

1 small to medium zucchini
   (around 7oz or 200g)

1 tbsp cashew, peanut, or
   almond butter

2 tbsp unsweetened cocoa
   powder

pinch of salt

½ tsp vanilla extract

¾ cup (180ml) nondairy milk
   (plus another ¼ cup/60ml,
   if needed)

4 to 5 soft dates (Deglet Noor
   preferred)

2 tsp ground flax seeds

1 tsp maple or agave syrup, or
   to taste (optional)

I know what you're thinking—I don't need vegetables in my milkshake, thank you very much! Hear me out! Raw, frozen zucchini is practically flavorless and gives this shake a level of creaminess similar to frozen banana, minus the overpowering flavor.

1 The night before, cut the zucchini into bite-size chunks. Let the chunks freeze overnight.

2 In a blender, add the zucchini, nut butter, cocoa powder, salt, vanilla, milk, dates, and flax seeds. Blend until smooth. If the consistency is a little too thick, adjust with more milk. Taste test! If you need it to be sweeter, add 1 teaspoon of maple or agave syrup. Serve immediately!

Tip: If your dates are on the dry side, no worries! The night before, place them in a small bowl, cover them with water, and let them soak in the fridge overnight. Alternatively, do this the day of with boiling water and let them soak for 10 to 15 minutes before adding them to the blender.

MY MOST FAVORITE SMOOTHIE BOWL

PREP TIME: 8 MINUTES
COOK TIME: NONE
YIELD: 1 SERVING

INGREDIENTS

1 cup (150g) frozen
    blueberries

frozen banana, cut into
    chunks

fresh banana, cut into chunks

1 tbsp peanut butter

1½ tbsp unsweetened cocoa
    powder

2 tsp ground flax seeds

¼ cup (60ml) orange juice

This thick and creamy smoothie bowl consists of a number of miscellaneous ingredients that work surprisingly well together. Like the title says, it's my favorite!

1   In a blender or food processor, add the blueberries, bananas, peanut butter, cocoa powder, flax seeds, and orange juice. Blend on high until smooth and thick. You may need to tamp down the ingredients while mixing, or add extra orange juice to allow for the mixture to combine properly.

2   Serve immediately with toppings of your choice! I love adding green apple chunks, berries, shredded coconut, and some type of crunchy granola. Try my **Peanut Butter Banana Bread Granola (page 37)**.

MINA'S MUESLI GUIDE

PREP TIME: 5 MINUTES
YIELD: 1 SERVING

INGREDIENTS

the BASE

3 to 5 tbsp oats (mix of old-
   fashioned and quick-cooking
   oats for added texture variety)

1 tsp semi-ground or ground flax
   seeds or hulled hemp seeds

dash of ground cinnamon (optional)

2 tbsp dried fruit of choice (raisins,
   cranberries, cherries, etc.)

the FRESHNESS

¼ to ½ cup (40 to 80g) fresh fruit,
   cut into chunks if necessary

the CRUNCH

¼ to ⅓ cup (30 to 40g) crunchy
   granola such as **Peanut Butter
   Banana Bread Granola (page 37)**

1 to 2 tbsp chopped nuts or
   sunflower seeds

the MILKINESS

cold nondairy milk or soy yogurt,
   to taste

extra toppings:

dusting of unsweetened cocoa
   powder

1 tbsp nut butter

1 tbsp cocoa nibs

1 tbsp chocolate chips

1 tbsp shredded coconut

1 tbsp puffed quinoa

1 tbsp vegan cookie crumbles

1 tbsp corn flakes

1 tbsp nuts

1 tbsp **Almond Chocolate Sauce
   (page 142)**

This is not a strict recipe, since muesli is so versatile. To me, muesli is the perfect meal. It can be a filling breakfast, a quick afternoon snack, or even lunch or dinner on those days you have absolutely no energy to cook.

1   Add the base ingredients to a bowl and give them a quick stir.

2   Next, add your fresh fruit, the crunchy items, and pour over the milk.

3   Lastly, add any extra toppings of choice.

Tip: I recommend a mix of sweet and sour fruits. A few tablespoons of freshly grated carrot is really good in this as well. Combine with cinnamon, walnuts, and vegan yogurt for some carrot cake muesli!

PERFECT PANCAKES

PREP TIME: 10 MINUTES
COOK TIME: 12 MINUTES
YIELD: 1 SERVING

INGREDIENTS

⅓ cup plus 2 tbsp (80ml plus 2 tbsp) nondairy milk, divided

1 tsp apple cider vinegar

3 tbsp unsweetened applesauce

½ tsp vanilla extract

½ cup plus 2½ tbsp (60g plus 2½ tbsp) white spelt flour or all-purpose flour

2½ tsp baking powder

1 to 2 tbsp sugar

pinch of salt

1 tsp coconut oil, for frying

Here is my mildly famous pancake recipe that's been tweaked and perfected over the years.

1 In a small bowl, combine ⅓ cup (80ml) of milk, vinegar, applesauce, and vanilla.

2 In a medium bowl, combine the flour, baking powder, sugar, and salt.

3 Pour in the milk mixture and stir until a thick batter forms. Consider adding up to 2 extra tablespoons of milk, as needed, for better consistency.

4 Heat the coconut oil in a nonstick skillet on medium. To cook each pancake, add 1 heaping tablespoon to ¼ cup (60ml) of batter to the skillet. I recommend using a metal ice cream scoop here as it releases the batter nicely and proportions it equally. Cook for 2 to 3 minutes on each side until golden brown and fluffy. Serve immediately.

Tip: I recommend serving these with some plant-based yogurt, fruit, nuts, and a generous drizzle of maple syrup.

CHICKPEA PANCAKES

PREP TIME: 10 MINUTES
COOK TIME: 12 MINUTES
YIELD: 1 SERVING

INGREDIENTS

½ cup (65g) chickpea flour

dash of curry powder

dash of smoked paprika

¼ tsp garlic powder

¼ tsp salt

¾ tsp baking powder

1½ tbsp nutritional yeast

½ cup (125ml) unsweetened
   nondairy milk

2 tsp apple cider vinegar

1 tsp coconut oil, for frying

optional toppings of choice:

1 to 2 tbsp vegan cream
   cheese

small handful of cherry
   tomatoes, quartered

1 green onion, chopped

2 pieces of vegan bacon
   (**page 91**), cooked and
   crumbled

Who said pancakes need to be sweet?

1   In a small bowl, mix together the chickpea flour, curry powder, smoked paprika, garlic powder, salt, baking powder, and yeast.

2   Add the nondairy milk and apple cider vinegar to the dry ingredients and mix until smooth. Set aside to rest for 5 minutes. Meanwhile, prepare your toppings.

3   Heat the coconut oil in a nonstick skillet on medium. Once hot, add 1 heaping tablespoon of batter per pancake and cook for 2 to 3 minutes on each side until golden brown. I recommend cooking 3 or 4 at a time. Serve immediately with your prepared serving options.

EVERYTHING BAGEL & KALE SUMMER ROLLS

PREP TIME: 18 MINUTES
COOK TIME: 7 MINUTES
YIELD: 1 TO 2 SERVINGS

INGREDIENTS

for the bagel seasoning:

2 tsp black sesame seeds

1 tbsp white sesame seeds

1 tsp poppy seeds

¼ tsp dried garlic (powdered or minced)

¼ tsp dried onion (powdered or minced)

¼ tsp salt (flaky salt preferred)

for the kale:

1 tbsp olive oil

2 cloves garlic, minced

3 to 4 small bunches of kale, (about 6oz/170g)*

1 tbsp lime or lemon juice

pinch of salt

for the rolls:

6 to 8 rice paper wrappers (around 15cm in diameter)

about ⅓ cup (65g) vegan cream cheese or vegan sour cream (alternatively use hummus)

3.5oz (100g) smoked tofu, cut into 3-in- (7-cm-) long sticks

1 small to medium carrot, cut into sticks, about 3in (7cm) long

2 tbsp soy sauce

These summer rolls can either be a tasty snack to share or a light, yet satisfying, breakfast for one. Dipping these in soy sauce is highly encouraged.

1   In a small bowl, combine all the spices for the bagel seasoning. Set aside.

2   Heat the olive oil in a medium saucepan on medium. Once hot, add the garlic and sauté for about 2 minutes.

3   Meanwhile, remove and discard the stems from the kale and cut the rest into rough chunks. Add the kale chunks and lime juice to the garlic. Cover with a lid. Let the kale steam for about 5 minutes. Once it looks slightly wilted, yet still nice and bright in color, add a pinch of salt. Stir and set aside.

4   Assemble the rolls! Fill a deep dish plate with room temperature water. Add one rice paper sheet. Let it soak in the water for 5 to 10 seconds, fully submerged.

5   Transfer the rice paper to a smooth work surface. The sheet will soften up as it sits. Add about 2 teaspoons of vegan cream cheese to the center of the rice paper, followed by 1 or 2 sticks of tofu, 1 or 2 carrot pieces, and a couple steamed kale leaves. Add a sprinkle of the bagel seasoning. Now the sheet should be soft enough to fold.

6   Roll the wraps like you would a burrito. Fold over the lower end of the rice paper, pulling the filling toward yourself. Then, fold over the sides. Finally, roll it up in the opposite direction, away from yourself (see **page 227** for steps).

7   Repeat steps 4 through 6 until all wraps have been folded, drying your working surface between each roll. Enjoy with some soy sauce.

Note:

*Kale with stems should weigh about 6oz (170g). Kale without stems should weigh about 4.3oz (120g).

GO-TO SCRAMBLED TOFU

PREP TIME: 6 MINUTES
COOK TIME: 15 MINUTES
YIELD: 1 SERVING

INGREDIENTS

7oz (200g) firm plain tofu

1½ tbsp cornstarch

pinch of salt

¼ tsp ground turmeric

¼ tsp ground black pepper

½ tsp dried oregano or other
  dried herbs of choice

1 tbsp nutritional yeast

1 tbsp white wine vinegar

2 tbsp unsweetened soy
  yogurt

½ tsp yellow mustard

1 small onion, finely chopped

vegetable oil, for frying

serving options:

kala namak

fresh parsley

green onion, chopped

cherry tomatoes, chopped

Ah yes, scrambled tofu—the classic vegan breakfast. Although, I'll take this any time of day!

1   Using your hands, crumble the tofu into a large mixing bowl. Add the cornstarch, salt, spices, herbs, and nutritional yeast. Mix well. Then, add the vinegar, soy yogurt, and mustard. Mix thoroughly.

2   Heat the vegetable oil in a nonstick skillet on medium. Sauté the onion for about 5 minutes until translucent. Then add the tofu mixture and let everything cook for another 5 to 8 minutes, stirring frequently.

3   For serving, sprinkle over a pinch of kala namak, some parsley, green onion, and tomatoes. I'd highly recommend serving this with some rice paper bacon (**page 91**).

CINNAMON RAISIN CORN BREAD

PREP TIME: 8 MINUTES
COOK TIME: 25 MINUTES
YIELD: 12 MUFFINS

INGREDIENTS

vegetable oil, for the pan

1 cup (250ml) nondairy milk

1 tbsp apple cider vinegar

½ cup minus 1 tbsp (100g)
   vegan butter

⅓ cup (85g) applesauce

2½ tbsp maple or agave
   syrup, plus more for serving

⅓ cup plus 1 tbsp (75g) sugar

1 cup (150g) cornmeal or
   polenta

1 cup (120g) all-purpose flour

2 tsp baking powder

1½ tsp ground cinnamon

1 tsp salt

⅓ cup (50g) raisins

serving options:

vegan butter

soy yogurt

peanut butter

almond butter

Since I'm from Europe, I had no idea what corn bread was until recently. But after making my own, I see the appeal! I mean, the buttery-ness? The satisfying texture from the cornmeal? My recipe comes with a cinnamon raisin flavor that adds a cozy sweetness to the mix.

1   Line a 12 cup muffin pan with muffin liners or lightly coat with vegetable oil. Preheat the oven to 350°F (180°C).

2   In a large bowl, add the milk and vinegar, stir, and set aside.

3   In a small saucepan on medium, add the butter, applesauce, syrup, and sugar. Cook until melted, about 2 minutes. Give this mixture a quick stir before adding it to the milk and vinegar, stirring as you pour. Set aside.

4   In a medium bowl, stir together the cornmeal, all-purpose flour, baking powder, cinnamon, and salt.

5   Add the flour mixture to the wet ingredient mixture and whisk until combined. Fold in the raisins.

6   Scoop the mix into the muffin cups, filling each ¾ full. Bake for 22 to 25 minutes. Let cool for 15 minutes. Serve warm with vegan butter, vegan yogurt, peanut butter, or almond butter and an optional drizzle of syrup.

Tip: I typically use polenta as a cornmeal substitute, as it is easier to find in Germany.

OVERNIGHT TOFU AVOCADO TOAST

PREP TIME: 6 MINUTES (PLUS
   OVERNIGHT MARINADE)
COOK TIME: 7 MINUTES
YIELD: 2 SERVINGS

INGREDIENTS

1½ tbsp soy sauce

1 tbsp white wine vinegar

2 to 3 tbsp nondairy milk

1 tbsp tomato paste/purée

1 tbsp agave or maple syrup

¼ tsp ground cumin

¾ tsp smoked paprika

7 ounces (200g) firm tofu, cut
   into chunks

1 small onion, finely chopped

vegetable oil, for pan

4 slices of bread

1 avocado, mashed

½ lemon

serving options:

1 to 2 tsp sesame seeds

1 to 2 tbsp chopped parsley

This classic avocado toast is topped with pan-fried, marinated tofu. So simple, yet so good!

1   Marinate the tofu the night before. In a medium glass jar at least 2 cups (500ml) in size, combine the soy sauce, vinegar, milk, tomato paste, syrup, cumin, and paprika. Mix well until it forms a thick, paste-like consistency.

2   Add the tofu and onion. Screw the lid on tight, and shake until the tofu is completely coated in the sauce. Refrigerate the jar overnight, or at least for 2 hours.

3   The next morning, heat the vegetable oil in a nonstick skillet on medium-high. Add the entire contents of the jar and let it cook for 6 to 8 minutes.

4   Meanwhile, toast the bread. Add an equal amount of mashed avocado and a squeeze of lemon juice to each slice of bread. Top each off with the tofu mixture. Perhaps add a sprinkle of sesame seeds and chopped parsley for finishing touches.

PEANUT SATAY TOAST

PREP TIME: 6 MINUTES
COOK TIME: 3 MINUTES
YIELD: 1 SERVING

Peanut butter and coconut come together in this recipe to create the most delicious toast experience.

INGREDIENTS

2 heaping tbsp natural
  peanut butter, preferably
  crunchy

1 tbsp soy sauce

½ cup (125ml) coconut milk

1 tbsp maple syrup

¼ tsp red pepper flakes, plus
  more for serving

pinch of salt

2 to 3 slices of bread

1¼ tbsp rice vinegar or
  lemon or lime juice

serving options:

cucumber, thinly sliced

radishes, thinly sliced

bell pepper, thinly sliced

raw carrot, cut into ribbons

1 tbsp fresh cilantro or
  parsley, roughly chopped

1 tsp sesame seeds

**5-Minute Cucumber Salad
  (page 125)**

1 In a small saucepan, add the peanut butter, soy sauce, coconut milk, syrup, red pepper flakes, and salt. Whisk well.

2 Bring the mixture close to a boil on medium-high. Reduce heat to low and let thicken for about 2 minutes, stirring frequently.

3 Meanwhile, toast your bread and gather your desired toppings.

4 Once the peanut mixture has thickened nicely, add in the vinegar. Mix well.

5 Top the toast with the peanut mixture and your serving options of choice. Enjoy!

FALAFEL CRUMBLE TACOS

PREP TIME: 12 MINUTES
COOK TIME: 10 MINUTES
YIELD: 6 TACOS, SERVES 2

Ever had a falafel-flavored breakfast taco? It's so good! And the crumbles are much easier to prepare than your classic deep fried falafel.

INGREDIENTS

1 14oz/400g can chickpeas, drained and rinsed

1 small red onion, quartered

2 cloves garlic, peeled

¼ tsp paprika

½ tsp ground cumin

2 tsp tahini

2 tbsp lemon juice

3 tbsp quick-cooking oats

1 to 2 handfuls of fresh parsley, chopped

pinch of salt, or to taste

pinch of ground black pepper, or to taste

1 tbsp vegetable oil, for pan

6 small tortillas (6in or 15cm), warmed

6 tbsp hummus

toppings of choice

serving options:

pickled vegetables

raw vegetables

hot sauce

Most Amazing Tahini Dressing (page 112)

parsley

sesame seeds

1   To make the falafel crumbles, in a food processor, add the chickpeas, onion, garlic, paprika, cumin, tahini, lemon juice, oats, parsley, salt, and black pepper. Pulse for just a few seconds, making sure the mixture stays chunky.

2   Heat the vegetable oil in a large nonstick skillet on medium. Once hot, add the chickpea mixture and, using a spatula, press it down firmly. Let the mix crisp up for 30 seconds to 1 minute, stir, then press it down again. Repeat this process 3 to 5 times until the mix is golden brown. Then, stir and toss the crumbles and allow them to cook for another 1 to 2 minutes.

3   Assemble the tacos! To the center of each warmed tortilla, add a tablespoon of hummus. Top that with a few tablespoons of the falafel crumbles and any serving options of choice. Enjoy!

PB&J FRENCH TOAST

This is probably the fanciest PB&J sandwich you'll ever encounter. It's covered in cornflakes, carefully pan-fried, and then baked to perfection.

....

PREP TIME: 15 MINUTES
COOK TIME: 20 MINUTES
YIELD: 2 SANDWICHES

....

INGREDIENTS

⅔ cup (160ml) nondairy milk

pinch of salt

¾ tsp baking powder

2 tsp sugar

2 tsp apple cider vinegar

1 tsp vanilla extract

2 tbsp cornstarch

4 slices of bread

peanut butter, to taste

jam of choice, to taste

2 tbsp coconut oil, divided

2 cups (75g) unsweetened cornflakes, divided

serving options:

1 to 2 tbsp powdered sugar

berries of choice

vegan cream or vegan yogurt

1 to 2 tbsp maple or rice syrup

1   In a shallow bowl wide enough to hold a slice of bread, thoroughly whisk together the nondairy milk, salt, baking powder, sugar, vinegar, vanilla, and cornstarch. Let sit for about 5 minutes.

2   Meanwhile, make your sandwiches. Spread 2 slices of bread with peanut butter and the other 2 with jam. I like a little more nut butter than jam, but use the ratio you like best. Combine the peanut butter slices with the jam slices to create 2 PB&J sandwiches.

3   Preheat the oven to 350°F (180°C) and line a baking sheet with parchment paper.

4   Heat 1 tablespoon of coconut oil in a large stainless steel or cast iron skillet on medium. During the frying process later, make sure the coconut oil doesn't smoke. If it does, lower the temperature a bit.

5   Transfer 1 cup (38g) of the cornflakes to a quarter-size plastic storage bag. Close the bag. Crush the flakes with your hands until the cornflakes are about ¼ the size they were before.

6   You are going to fry one sandwich at a time. Place the bowl with the milk mixture next to your stove. Dip the first sandwich into the milk bowl. Allow to soak for a few seconds, flip it, then allow to soak for a few more seconds.

7   Transfer the soaked sandwich to the bag and close it. Cover the sandwich in the crushed cornflakes, pressing down onto the bread with your hands, making as many flakes stick to the bread as possible. Some are going to fall off, but that's okay.

8   Carefully transfer the coated bread from the bag to the hot pan. Fry the sandwich for about 2 minutes on each side or until golden brown. Toward the end of the cooking process, press down lightly onto the bread with a spatula. Now transfer the fried sandwich to the lined baking sheet.

9   Wipe down the pan, getting rid of any lost cornflakes. Repeat steps 4 to 8 with the second sandwich.

10 Bake the fried sandwiches for 10 minutes. Serve with the options of your choice. The gooey inside will be very hot, so be careful. Enjoy!

COCONUT RICE BUNS

PREP TIME: 10 MINUTES (PLUS RICE
    SOAKING AND RISING TIME)
COOK TIME: 25 MINUTES
YIELD: 9 BUNS

The dough here is made using rice that's first soaked and then blended together with a few other ingredients, resulting in fluffy little buns that come with a hint of sweet coconut flavor.

INGREDIENTS

1 cup (200g) short grain rice

⅓ cup (80ml) boiling water, plus more for soaking rice

⅓ cup (80ml) cold nondairy milk*

2½ tbsp sugar

1¼ tsp dry active yeast

1 tbsp vegan butter, for greasing

⅓ cup (30g) shredded coconut

½ tsp salt

1½ tbsp vegetable oil

serving options:

vegan butter

jam of choice

vegan yogurt

fresh fruit of choice

1 The night before, in a large pot, add the rice and pour over boiling water until the rice is completely covered. Cover with a lid and let rest for 8 hours.

2 In a small bowl, combine the ⅓ cup boiling water, cold milk, and sugar. Sprinkle over the yeast and let sit for 10 minutes in a warm, protected area.

3 In the meantime, coat a 9 cup muffin pan with vegan butter and set aside.

4 Drain the rice using a fine strainer. Give the rice a quick rinse. Then, add it to a blender along with the coconut, salt, oil, and yeast mixture. Blend until smooth. Once smooth, continue blending for an additional 30 seconds to 1 minute.

5 Pour the contents into the muffin cups, dividing evenly. Do not fill the molds higher than ¾ of the way. Place the muffin pan in a warm, protected area and allow the buns to rise for 40 to 45 minutes.

6 Toward the end of the rising process, preheat the oven to 375°F (190°C). Bake for 25 minutes, or until golden brown.

7 Let cool for about 15 minutes before removing from the pan. Carefully run a butter knife along the edges before lifting out each bun.

8 Serve immediately with jam and vegan butter or vegan yogurt and fresh fruit. Store in an airtight container at room temperature for up to 2 days. Do not keep these in the fridge, as they will dry out too quickly.

Tip: After 1 to 2 days, these buns will seem dry and stale. Microwave them for 20 to 30 seconds to revive them.

Note:

  *I recommend light coconut milk for a more coconutty flavor. I do not recommend full fat coconut milk.

OVERNIGHT OAT & SEED BREAD

PREP TIME: 5 MINUTES (PLUS
     OVERNIGHT SOAK TIME)
COOK TIME: 85 MINUTES
YIELD: 1 LOAF (10 TO 12 SLICES)

Calling all pumpkin seed lovers! This no-yeast bread is for you! Also, who can spot the unintentional vegan symbol in the photo?

INGREDIENTS

3 cups (270g) old-fashioned
     oats

1½ cups (180g) pumpkin
     seeds

½ cup (70g) sunflower seeds

2 tbsp sesame seeds

⅓ cup (37g) ground flax
     seeds

1½ tbsp chia seeds, or
     substitute with additional
     flax seeds

2 tsp salt

2 cups (500ml) water

serving options:

vegan cream cheese

hummus

vegan butter

cherry tomatoes

parsely

cucumber slices

Vegan Tzatziki (page 114)

1   The night before, in a large bowl, combine the oats, seeds, and salt. Add the water and stir. Cover the bowl and leave in the fridge overnight.

2   The next day, line an 8-in (20-cm) loaf pan with wet parchment paper. Make sure you leave parchment paper hanging over the sides of the pan to make it easier to lift out later.

3   Using your hands,* knead the soaked oat mix for about 1 minute. Then, add the dough to the prepared loaf pan, pressing it down firmly. Smooth the top until flat. Place the pan into the unheated oven. Next, heat the oven to 400°F (200°C) and bake for 85 minutes.

4   Remove from the pan and let cool completely on the counter before slicing. Serve with your preferred toppings. Enjoy!

Note:

*This is going to be quite cold on your fingers, so, alternatively, give this a thorough mix using an electric mixer with a hook attachment.

HOT ORANGE WAFFLES

PREP TIME: 15 MINUTES
COOK TIME: 20 MINUTES
YIELD: 6 TO 8 WAFFLES

These waffles topped with luxurious orange syrup are my favorite. They may look fancy, but they're super easy to make.

INGREDIENTS

vegetable oil, for waffle iron

vegan whipped cream

raspberries

for the waffle batter:

1 cup (250ml) nondairy milk

1 tsp vanilla extract

⅓ cup (80g) applesauce

1 tbsp apple cider vinegar

1¾ cup (210g) all-purpose flour

3 tsp baking powder

¼ tsp salt

1½ tbsp cornstarch

6 tbsp powdered sugar

for the orange sauce:

1 orange

½ cup (125ml) orange juice

2 tbsp sugar

1 tbsp vegan butter

1 tsp cornstarch

2 tbsp water

1 For the waffle batter, in a large bowl, combine the milk, vanilla, applesauce, and vinegar. Set aside to curdle for a bit. In a separate small bowl, mix the flour, baking powder, salt, cornstarch, and powdered sugar.

2 Add the dry ingredients to the wet ingredients and stir until combined. Be careful not to overmix. Let the batter rest while you prepare the orange sauce.

3 Using a fine grater, zest the orange directly into a small saucepan, until you have collected about 1 teaspoon of zest. Next, add the orange juice, sugar, and butter to the saucepan.

4 In a small glass or bowl, combine the cornstarch and water until no clumps remain. Add this mixture to the saucepan as well, and stir.

5 Bring to a boil on high. Reduce heat to medium and let simmer for about 2 minutes, stirring thoroughly until a syrup-like consistency has been achieved.

6 Optional: Cut the zested orange into small, thin slices and set aside for serving.

7 To cook the waffles, coat a waffle iron with vegetable oil. Heat to medium-high. Add batter to the waffle iron according to appliance instructions. Close it and let the waffle cook for 3 to 4 minutes, or until golden brown. Waffle makers can differ, so adjust the cook time to how crispy you prefer your waffles.

8 Serve with the hot orange sauce, orange slices, vegan whipped cream, and raspberries. Enjoy!

Tip: These waffles freeze nicely and can be easily reheated in the toaster.

LUNCH

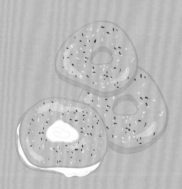

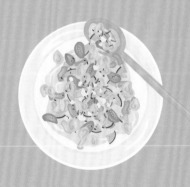

TERIYAKI BRUSSELS SPROUT WRAPS

PREP TIME: 15 MINUTES
COOK TIME: 12 MINUTES
YIELD: 4 WRAPS

INGREDIENTS

12oz (300g) Brussels sprouts

1 tbsp cornstarch

⅓ cup plus 2 tbsp (80ml plus 2 tbsp) water, divided

1 tbsp soy sauce

2½ tbsp brown rice, maple, or agave syrup

1 tbsp miso paste

3 tbsp balsamic vinegar

2 cloves garlic, peeled and minced

1-inch piece ginger, minced

1 tbsp olive oil, for skillet

pinch of chili flakes

pinch of salt

½ tsp lemon zest

4 tbsp vegan cream cheese or hummus

4 (10-in/25-cm) tortillas

1 avocado, thinly sliced

1 carrot, cut into ribbons using a vegetable peeler

⅓ cucumber, cut into sticks

2 tsp roasted sesame seeds (optional)

romaine lettuce or fresh spinach (optional)

Who knew eating your veggies could be this tasty?

1 Bring a small or medium pot of water to a boil. Meanwhile, remove the stems of the Brussels sprouts and cut each one in half. If needed, discard a few of the outer leaves that might fall off.

2 Boil the Brussels sprouts for about 4 minutes, then drain. Shake off any excess water. Pat them dry, if necessary.

3 In a small glass or bowl, combine the cornstarch and 2 tablespoons of water until no clumps remain.

4 In a small saucepan, add the soy sauce, syrup, miso paste, vinegar, ⅓ cup (80ml) water, garlic, ginger, and the cornstarch solution. Stir. Bring to a boil on high while stirring continuously. Reduce heat to medium and let simmer for about 2 minutes, or until thickened. Set aside.

5 Heat the olive oil in a large skillet on medium-high. Once hot, add the drained Brussels sprouts. Cook them for about 6 minutes, stirring frequently so all sides brown evenly. Season with chili flakes, salt, and lemon zest.

6 Now add the teriyaki sauce to the sprouts. Stir, then set aside.

7 To build your wraps, add a tablespoon of cream cheese or hummus to the center of each tortilla, then a couple tbsp of the Brussels sprouts mixture, a few avocado slices, a few carrot ribbons, and 1 or 2 cucumber sticks. Consider adding some sesame seeds and greens as well!

8 Roll up the tortillas. Fold the end closest to you over the filling and pull the filling back toward you. Fold the left and right sides inward and then continue rolling it away from you. Repeat until all wraps have been rolled.

9 Heat a nonstick skillet on medium-high. Add the wraps, open side down, and crisp for 1 to 2 minutes on each side. Enjoy!

EGG SALAD LETTUCE WRAPS

PREP TIME: 5 MINUTES
COOK TIME: 15 MINUTES
YIELD: 3 TO 4 SERVINGS

INGREDIENTS

1½ cups (180g) short cut
  pasta (penne, rigatoni, etc.)

¾ cup (120g) chickpeas,
  drained and rinsed

1 to 2 romaine lettuce hearts
  (about 12 leaves)

drizzle of hot sauce, for
  serving (optional)

for the dressing:

1¼ tbsp white wine vinegar

1 tbsp minced dill

2 tbsp minced chives*

3 tbsp vegan mayonnaise

3 tbsp thick unsweetened soy
  yogurt

¼ tsp kala namak (plus a
  pinch for serving)

¼ tsp salt (plus more, to
  taste)

¼ tsp ground black pepper

¼ tsp ground turmeric

2 tsp mustard

Now this is the kind of meal you want to impress your parents with! The egg texture is brought to you by a mixture of chickpeas and cooked pasta, and the authentic flavor comes from the use of black salt.

1 Cook the pasta according to package instructions. After draining the pasta, give it a quick rinse with cold water to bring down the temperature a bit.

2 Meanwhile, in a large bowl, combine the vinegar, dill, chives, mayonnaise, yogurt, kala namak, salt, black pepper, turmeric, and mustard. Mix until a smooth dressing forms.

3 Drain and rinse the chickpeas. Add the chickpeas and pasta to a food processor and pulse for a few seconds until slightly broken up.

4 Transfer the pasta chickpea mix to the large bowl with the dressing. Mix well. You may want to add more salt and spices, to taste.

5 Serve the salad in the lettuce leaves with a sprinkle of kala namak and, optionally, a small drizzle of your favorite hot sauce.

Note:
*Chives are best cut with kitchen scissors.

PINK BULGUR BOWL WITH CRISPY TOFU BITES

PREP TIME: 30 MINUTES (PLUS 1
HOUR FOR TZATZIKI RECIPE)
COOK TIME: 25 MINUTES
YIELD: 2 TO 3 SERVINGS

INGREDIENTS

4 to 6 tbsp **Vegan Tzatziki**
(**page 114**) or store-bought
hummus

for the pink bulgur:

⅔ cup (130g) medium, coarse
bulgur wheat

1⅓ cups (320ml) water

1 cooked red beet

1 tbsp lemon juice

1 tbsp olive oil

salt, to taste

ground black pepper, to taste

for the tofu:

1 (7oz/200g) block firm plain
tofu, cut into cubes

2 tbsp all-purpose flour

dash of curry powder

dash of garlic powder

dash of paprika

pinch of salt

dash of ground black pepper

1 to 2 tbsp vegetable oil, for
frying

1 to 2 tbsp white wine

1 tbsp maple syrup

1 tbsp soy sauce

optional add-ins:

¾ cup (95g) frozen edamame,
boiled for 2 minutes

¼ cucumber, cut into thin
slices

1 medium carrot, cut into
ribbons**

roasted sesame seeds

A vibrant bowl that's almost too pretty to eat.

1   Prepare the **Vegan Tzatziki (page 114)** ahead of time, unless
you are using hummus.

2   In a medium pot, add the bulgur wheat and water and cover
with a lid. Bring to a boil on high. Reduce the heat to medium-
low and let simmer for about 15 minutes or until the liquid is
fully absorbed.* Keeping the lid on, remove from the heat and
let the bulgur sit for 5 to 10 minutes to fully soften.

3   To make the tofu, in a medium bowl, combine the tofu, flour,
curry powder, garlic powder, papika, salt, and black pepper.

4   Heat the vegetable oil in a nonstick skilled on medium-high.
Once hot, add the tofu and let it crisp up for about
5 minutes, flipping the tofu cubes every 30 seconds or so to
achieve a golden brown color on all sides.

5   Next, add the white wine, maple syrup, and soy sauce to the
tofu. Let this cook for another 2 minutes, stirring often until
the tofu gets a bit darker in color and starts to crisp up again.

6   Add the beet to a food processor and pulse it into small
shreds. Alternatively, use a cheese grater or a knife to cut the
beet into fine strips. Add the beet pieces to the pot of bulgur,
together with the lemon juice, olive oil, salt, and black pepper.
Mix well.

7   To plate, divide the tofu, bulgur, tzatziki, and optional add-ins
between 2 or 3 bowls. Enjoy!

Notes:
*Keep an eye on the pot. Toward the beginning of the cooking process, the
water might start to overflow. Simply lift the lid for a few seconds when you
feel like this is about to happen. Repeat as needed.

I highly recommend giving the carrots a quick pickle. Check out **page 96 for
the instructions.

ULTIMATE VEGAN GRILLED CHEESE

PREP TIME: 10 MINUTES
COOK TIME: 10 MINUTES
YIELD: 1 SANDWICH

INGREDIENTS

2 slices of bread

1 to 2 tsp vegan butter

2 tsp ketchup or marinara sauce (optional)

1 tbsp cornstarch

1 tbsp nutritional yeast

¼ cup (30g) tapioca starch

generous pinch of salt

¼ tsp garlic powder

pinch of ground turmeric, for color

½ cup (125ml) nondairy milk

2 tsp vegan butter

2 tsp white wine vinegar

¼ cup (25g) shredded vegan cheese* (optional, but recommended)

The title sums up this recipe pretty well. The cheese is made with a starch-based sauce that is naturally stringy and gooey, giving it that authentic grilled cheese pull we're all looking for.

1   Spread vegan butter on one side of each piece of bread. Add any optional ketchup or marinara sauce to the unbuttered side of one slice.

2   In a small saucepan combine the cornstarch, nutritional yeast, tapioca starch, salt, garlic powder, and turmeric. Next, add the milk, mixing thoroughly with a whisk as you pour.

3   Place the saucepan on medium-high and, once up to temperature, add the butter, white wine vinegar, and optional vegan cheese. Using a wooden spoon, mix well. Let cook for about 2 minutes, stirring throughout, until a thick, stretchy mass of cheese forms.

4   Transfer this mix to the unbuttered side of one slice of bread. Top with the second piece of bread, buttered side facing outward.

5   Heat a medium skillet on medium. Once hot, add the sandwich. Grill for 2 to 3 minutes on each side, pressing it down a little with a spatula as it cooks.

Tip: If your bread slices are on the small side, you can easily make 2 small sandwiches with the cheese mix!

Note:

*The cheese needs to be able to melt. Not all vegan cheeses melt, unfortunately.

LEMON ZOODLE TOAST

PREP TIME: 6 MINUTES
COOK TIME: 10 MINUTES
YIELD: 1 TO 2 SERVINGS

INGREDIENTS

1 to 2 zucchinis

vegetable oil, for frying

pinch of salt

¼ tsp garlic powder, or to taste

½ tsp fresh lemon zest

2 to 4 slices of bread, toasted

2 to 4 tbsp hummus or vegan cream cheese

1 to 2 tsp nutritional yeast

pinch of red pepper flakes

1 to 2 tsp sesame seeds

Lemon zest makes everything better. This simple, yet fancy toast is no exception to that rule.

1 Using a vegetable peeler, cut the zucchini into ribbons.

2 Heat the vegetable oil in a nonstick skillet on medium-high. Once hot, add the zucchini and cook for about 8 minutes. Season with salt, garlic powder, and lemon zest.

3 Spread each piece of toast with 1 tablespoon of hummus or vegan cream cheese and top with the zucchini "noodles."

4 Sprinkle over the nutritional yeast, red pepper flakes, and sesame seeds. Enjoy!

GREEN PEA TOAST

PREP TIME: 5 MINUTES
COOK TIME: 5 MINUTES
YIELD: 2 SERVINGS

INGREDIENTS

¼ cup (60ml) olive oil

pinch of chili flakes

2 to 3 cloves garlic, roughly
chopped

2 cups (270g) frozen peas

1 tbsp nutritional yeast

1 tbsp lemon juice, or to taste

½ tsp salt, or to taste

pinch of ground black
pepper, or to taste

4 slices of bread, toasted

toppings of choice

You want something other than plain hummus on toast for once? Try this colorful and super versatile green pea spread.

1 In a small pot or skillet on medium, add the olive oil, chili flakes, and garlic. Sauté until garlic is a light golden brown, for 1 to 2 minutes. Add the frozen peas, nutritional yeast, lemon juice, salt, and black pepper. Let cook for an additional 2 to 3 minutes.

2 Transfer to a food processor and blend until smooth. Add additional lemon juice, salt, or black pepper as needed.

3 Serve atop the toast. Perhaps add some cherry tomatoes and hemp seeds. The spread can be refrigerated in an airtight container for up to 3 days.

Tip: This can be used in many other recipes! Try it with the **Burrito-Style Oats (page 29)** or the **Green Pea Pasta Salad (page 84).**

GREEN PEA PASTA SALAD

PREP TIME: 8 MINUTES
COOK TIME: 15 MINUTES
YIELD: 2 SERVINGS

INGREDIENTS

1½ cups (180g) pasta of
   choice

¼ cup (60ml) olive oil

pinch of chili flakes

2 to 3 cloves garlic, roughly
   chopped

2 cups (270g) frozen peas

¼ cup (60ml) vegetable broth

¼ cup (60ml) reserved pasta
   water

1 tbsp nutritional yeast

1 tbsp lemon juice, or to taste

½ tsp salt, or to taste

¼ tsp ground black pepper,
   or to taste

2 handfuls of fresh baby
   spinach or arugula

¼ to ½ cup (40 to 80g) cherry
   or sun-dried tomatoes,
   chopped

¼ cup (30g) walnuts,
   chopped

As you see here, the green pea spread from the previous recipe can be more than just a toast topping.

1   Prepare the pasta according to package instructions. Drain the pasta, reserving ¼ cup (60ml) of the pasta water. Set aside.

2   In a small pot or skillet over medium heat, add the olive oil, chili flakes, and garlic. Sauté until garlic is a light golden brown, for 1 to 2 minutes. Add the frozen peas. Then, add the broth, pasta water, yeast, lemon juice, salt, and black pepper. Cook for another 2 to 3 minutes.

3   Transfer to a food processor and blend until a creamy sauce forms. Scrape down the sides a few times as you blend, if necessary.

4   In a large bowl, bring together the pasta, green pea sauce, spinach, tomatoes, and walnuts. If needed, add some extra lemon juice, black pepper, or salt. Serve and enjoy!

RED PESTO QUINOA

PREP TIME: 10 MINUTES
COOK TIME: 20 MINUTES
YIELD: 3 SERVINGS

INGREDIENTS

1⅓ cup (240g) quinoa

2⅓ cup (580ml) plus ¼ cup (60ml) water, divided

⅓ cup (50g) cashews

5.3oz (150g) oil-packed sun-dried tomatoes*

1 tbsp red or white wine vinegar

⅓ cup (80ml) olive oil

1 tbsp nutritional yeast

⅓ tsp salt, plus more to taste

¼ tsp ground black pepper

1 clove garlic, peeled

¼ cup (5g) basil

½ cup (12g) arugula, chopped

¼ cup (40g) cherry tomatoes, chopped

Yeah, we've all heard of pesto pasta. But have you ever had pesto quinoa? This is quite the underrated food combination, in my opinion.

1　Preheat the oven to 400°F (200°C) and line a baking sheet with parchment paper.

2　Using a fine mesh strainer, rinse the quinoa. In a medium to large pot, add quinoa and 2⅓ cup (580ml) water, cover, and bring to a boil on high. Reduce heat to medium and let simmer for 15 to 20 minutes, or until the water has been absorbed. Remove from the heat and allow to sit, covered, for 5 to 10 minutes, or until soft.

3　Meanwhile, place the cashews on the baking sheet in a single layer and bake for about 8 minutes until golden brown.

4　Add the roasted cashews, sun-dried tomatoes, vinegar, olive oil, yeast, salt, black pepper, garlic, basil, and remaining ¼ cup (60ml) of water to a food processor. Blend until you're left with smooth pesto.

5　Combine the quinoa, pesto, arugula, and cherry tomatoes. Taste and adjust the seasoning, if needed.

Note:

*If your tomatoes come with excess oil, use it and supplement with the olive oil until you have ⅓ cup (80ml). It is important you do not exceed ⅓ cup (80ml) of oil in this recipe.

GRILLED CAESAR SALAD LETTUCE STEAKS

PREP TIME: 10 MINUTES
COOK TIME: 10 MINUTES
YIELD: 2 SERVINGS (SERVES 4 AS A
  SIDE)

INGREDIENTS

2 romaine lettuce hearts

vegetable oil, for pan

2 slices of bread, cut into
  bite-size chunks

for the cashew Parmesan:

1 cup (140g) cashews

1 tsp salt

1 to 2 tbsp nutritional yeast

¼ tsp garlic powder

¼ tsp onion powder

for the Caesar dressing:

2 tbsp room temperature
  vegan cream cheese or
  hummus

½ tsp mustard

1 tsp olive oil

1 tbsp white wine vinegar

1 tbsp caper brine

1 tsp capers

1 tbsp vegan Worcestershire
  sauce

1 to 2 tbsp water, if needed

salt, to taste

ground black pepper, to taste

Not many people know you can grill lettuce! The grilling gives the romaine a smoky, hearty flavor that's similar to crispy Brussels sprouts—and in combination with Caesar salad dressing plus homemade croutons? Heaven.

1   To make the Parmesan, add the cashews, salt, yeast, garlic powder, and onion powder to a food processor and blend until fine. Set aside.

2   To prepare the Caesar dressing, in a small bowl, whisk together the vegan cream cheese, 3 tablespoons of the cashew Parmesan, mustard, olive oil, vinegar, caper brine, capers, and Worcestershire sauce. Adjust the consistency with 1 to 2 tablespoons of water, as needed. Add salt and black pepper, to taste. Set aside.

3   Trim the romaine hearts, leaving most of the stem intact to ensure the leaves stay together when frying. Cut the romaine hearts in half lengthwise.

4   Heat vegetable oil in a large grill or sauté pan over medium-high. Once hot, add the romaine hearts. You may need to do this in batches. Grill for 2 to 3 minutes on each side until lightly charred grill marks appear. Rest the grilled lettuce on a plate until all have been cooked.

5   Turn the heat down to medium, and add more vegetable oil. Add the bread chunks and toast them for 2 to 3 minutes until browned and crispy.

6   Now serve! Assemble two grilled lettuce halves per plate. Lightly sprinkle each lettuce half with salt and black pepper. Add half the croutons to each plate. Top this off with the dressing and more of the parmesan. Enjoy!

Tip: There will be Parmesan left over. Consider saving it for another recipe, such as the **Pasta À La Vino (page 156)**. It can be refrigerated for up to two weeks.

BBQ COUSCOUS SALAD

PREP TIME: 15 MINUTES
COOK TIME: 10 MINUTES
YIELD: 2 SERVINGS

INGREDIENTS

¾ cup (180ml) water

1 to 2 tsp olive oil

pinch of salt

¾ cup (135g) dried couscous

⅔ cup (120g) cherry
  tomatoes, halved

2 large handfuls of fresh
  greens of choice

2 tbsp sunflower seeds

for the rice paper bacon:

2 tbsp vegan barbecue sauce

1 tsp white wine vinegar

1 tsp vegetable oil

½ tsp mustard

2 rice paper wrappers
  (around 6in/15cm in length
  or diameter)

for the dressing:

1 tbsp white wine vinegar

1½ tbsp vegan sour cream or
  thick, unsweetened soy
  yogurt

1 tbsp vegan mayonnaise

salt, to taste, if needed

ground black pepper, to taste,
  if needed

A fancy, yet hearty bowl made with homemade rice paper bacon and covered in a delicious pink dressing.

1 Preheat the oven to 400°F (200°C) and line a baking sheet with parchment paper.

2 In a small bowl, combine the barbecue sauce, white wine vinegar, vegetable oil, and mustard. Set aside.

3 Fill a deep dish plate with room temperature water. Let a sheet of rice paper soak in the water for 3 to 5 seconds to soften up a bit. Using kitchen scissors, cut the paper into strips about 1in (3cm) wide. Transfer strips to the baking sheet. Repeat with the second sheet of rice paper.

4 Brush each strip with the barbecue marinade. Brush vertically, going over the edges. Reserve approximately one tablespoon of the marinade and set aside.

5 Bake the strips for 6 to 8 minutes until crispy and deep orange-red in color. Keep an eye on it as the bacon can burn quickly.

6 Meanwhile, in a small saucepan, add the water, olive oil, and salt and bring to a boil on high. Once boiling, stir in the couscous. Remove from the heat. Set aside for 6 to 10 minutes to allow the couscous to absorb the water.

7 To make the dressing, in a small bowl add the vinegar, sour cream, mayonnaise, salt, and black pepper to the small bowl with the remaining barbecue marinade. Mix until smooth.

8 Time to assemble! Divide the couscous, tomatoes and greens between two bowls or deep dish plates. Crumble the bacon and add it in. Top that off with the dressing. Finish with a sprinkle of sunflower seeds. Alternatively, mix all the components at once. Think of this like shaking a salad in a container. Divide between two plates and enjoy!

Tip: After steaming the couscous, rather than stirring it with a wooden spoon, use a fork. This ensures the couscous stays fluffy!

SIMPLE BEAN TOAST

PREP TIME: 5 MINUTES
COOK TIME: 15 MINUTES
YIELD: 1 TO 2 SERVINGS

INGREDIENTS

½ cup (110g) rinsed kidney
   or black beans

1 tbsp vegan mayonnaise

1 tsp mustard

1 tbsp lemon juice

1 tsp agave or maple syrup

pinch of salt

2 to 3 slices of bread

spices of choice, to taste:

onion powder

garlic powder

paprika

chili flakes

serving options:

cucumber, sliced into cubes

cherry tomatoes, halved

½ avocado, sliced

sprinkle of sesame seeds

pickled onions

hot sauce

It's beans on toast. Literally.

1   Preheat the oven to 400°F (200°C).

2   In a medium bowl or deep dish plate, mash the beans well. Add the mayonnaise, mustard, lemon juice, syrup, salt, and spices of choice, to taste. Mix well.

3   Place 2 or 3 slices of bread onto a baking sheet. Top each slice of bread with an equal amount of bean mixture. Bake for 12 to 15 minutes or until the top is set and lightly browned and the bottom of the bread is crispy.

4   Top with any of the listed serving options, or get creative and add your own. Enjoy!

GO-TO CHICKPEA SALAD

PREP TIME: 6 MINUTES
COOK TIME: 3 MINUTES
YIELD: 2 SERVINGS

INGREDIENTS

¼ cup (35g) chopped
   cashews or pine nuts

½ medium cucumber, cut
   into cubes

7oz (200g) cherry tomatoes,
   quartered

1 handful of fresh greens of
   choice, roughly chopped
   (optional)

1 (14oz/400g) can chickpeas,
   drained and rinsed

2 tsp nutritional yeast

2 tbsp chopped parsley

for the dressing:

3 tbsp plain soy yogurt

1½ tbsp white tahini

1 tbsp white wine vinegar

pinch of curry powder

dash of paprika

dash of garlic powder

dash of cumin

pinch of salt, or to taste

This is the perfect salad to quickly whip up during a quick home office lunch break. Or prepare it the night before to take with you! Served with a tortilla or bread on the side, this makes for a super satisfying meal.

1   Heat a small, dry skillet on medium-high. Add the nuts and let them toast for about 3 minutes, occasionally stirring, until they become golden brown and fragrant. Set aside.

2   To prepare the dressing, in a medium bowl combine the yogurt, tahini, vinegar, curry powder, paprika, garlic powder, cumin, and salt. Mix well.

3   Add the cucumber, tomatoes, optional greens, and chickpeas to the dressing bowl. Mix well.

4   Divide the salad between two bowls. Sprinkle the toasted nuts, nutritional yeast, and parsley over top. Enjoy!

BANH–MI STYLE SALAD

PREP TIME: 20 MINUTES (PLUS
   1 HOUR PICKLE TIME)
COOK TIME: 20 MINUTES
YIELD: 2 SERVINGS

This salad contains all the components you'd find in a tasty tofu banh mi. The tofu is prepared in a way that makes it taste like coconut chicken!

INGREDIENTS

⅓ of a baguette

2 romaine lettuce hearts, roughly chopped

½ cucumber, cut into chunks

¼ cup (about 5g) cilantro

1 to 2 tbsp roasted sesame seeds

for the quick-pickled carrots:

1 to 2 medium carrots

⅔ cup (160ml) water

½ cup (125ml) white wine vinegar

2 tbsp agave or maple syrup

1 tsp salt

for the tofu:

7oz (200g) firm plain tofu

1½ tbsp cornstarch

2 tsp nutritional yeast

2 tsp soy sauce

1½ tbsp lime juice

¼ tsp salt

½ tsp onion powder

¼ tsp garlic powder

¼ tsp chili flakes, or to taste

1 tbsp vegetable oil

¼ cup (60ml) coconut milk

for the dressing:

1½ tbsp vegan mayo

1 tbsp ketchup

½ tsp sriracha

2 tsp lime juice or rice vinegar

1 tsp soy sauce

1. To make the pickled vegetables, using a vegetable peeler, cut the carrots into ribbons. Transfer them to a large jar. Add the water, vinegar, syrup, and salt. Screw the lid on tight and shake well. Refrigerate for at least an hour.

2. Cut the baguette into bite-size chunks.

3. Heat a dry, nonstick skillet without oil on medium-high. Once hot, add the baguette chunks and toast them for 2 to 3 minutes, until crispy. Set aside.

4. Over a medium bowl, using your hands, crumble up the tofu into bite-size pieces. Add the cornstarch, yeast, soy sauce, lime juice, salt, and spices. Mix well.

5. Now grab the nonstick pan you just used for the bread and wipe clean with a paper towel. Heat the vegetable oil on medium-high. Once hot, add the tofu mixture. Cook for 6 to 8 minutes, or until golden brown and crispy. Then, pour the coconut milk over top. Let the tofu continue to cook for 2 to 3 minutes until the milk has been fully absorbed.

6. For the dressing, in a small bowl, mix together the vegan mayo, ketchup, sriracha, lime juice, and soy sauce.

7. Divide the chopped lettuce, cucumber, pickled vegetables, croutons, and cooked tofu between two large plates. Drizzle the dressing over top. Finish off with chopped cilanto and sesame seeds. Enjoy!

QUICK CARROT & GLASS NOODLE SALAD

PREP TIME: 10 MINUTES
COOK TIME: 6 MINUTES
YIELD: 3 SERVINGS

When you don't feel like cooking, glass noodles really are a lifesaver.

INGREDIENTS

1 medium carrot, cut into ribbons using a vegetable peeler

4oz (100g) dried glass noodles (also known as vermicelli or cellophane noodles)

¼ cup (15g) cilantro, thai basil leaves, or parsley, chopped

1 to 2 green onions, sliced

1¼ cups (90g) shredded white, red, or napa cabbage

4 tbsp crispy fried onion

2 to 3 tbsp roasted sesame seeds

for the dressing:

3 tbsp soy sauce

3 tbsp lime juice, or more to taste

1½ tbsp maple syrup

1½ tsp sesame oil

1½ tbsp olive oil

1 to 2 cloves garlic, minced

pinch of chili flakes, or to taste

pinch of salt, if needed

1 Add the carrot ribbons and glass noodles to a large bowl. Pour in boiling water until the noodles are completely submerged and let sit, covered, for about 6 minutes, or until the glass noodles are tender.

2 To prepare the dressing, in a small bowl, stir together the soy sauce, lime juice, maple syrup, sesame oil, olive oil, garlic, and chili flakes.

3 Drain the noodles and carrots and return them to the large bowl. Add the cilantro, green onion, and cabbage. Pour the dressing over top and mix well.*

4 Lastly, add the crispy fried onion and sesame seeds. Mix once more. Add salt or lime juice, if needed. Enjoy!

Tip: This salad keeps fresh in the fridge for up to 2 days. Consider preparing it the night before to save time. Purchase pre-shredded cabbage for an even quicker prepping process.

Note:
*Use 2 wooden spoons here to mix the salad. Lift and fold the contents of the bowl, so as not to break the noodles.

SUN-DRIED TOMATO BAKED OATS

PREP TIME: 5 MINUTES
COOK TIME: 30 MINUTES
YIELD: 2 SERVINGS

To me, these salty oat cakes taste of focaccia, pizza, and summer.

INGREDIENTS

2 tsp olive oil, for greasing

1 cup (90g) quick-cooking oats

½ tsp salt

½ tsp garlic powder

1 tsp baking powder

1 tbsp nutritional yeast

3½ tbsp unsweetened applesauce

½ cup (125ml) water

2 tbsp olive oil

½ cup (50g) oil-packed sun-dried tomatoes, diced

serving options:

cherry tomatoes

fresh herbs

Garden Veggie Jalapeño Dip (page 116)

vegan feta

vegan cream cheese

avocado

hummus

fresh arugula

nuts and seeds

1 Lightly coat two 6 or 8 oz (180ml or 240ml) ramekins with 1 teaspoon of olive oil each. You can also use any excess oil from the tomatoes for this. Preheat the oven to 350°F (180°C).

2 In a blender or food processor add the oats, salt, garlic powder, baking powder, nutritional yeast, applesauce, water, and olive oil. Instead of the olive oil, you could use excess oil from the sun-dried tomatoes. Blend until smooth.

3 Then, add the sun-dried tomato pieces and blend a few moments more to distribute the tomatoes evenly in the batter.

4 Divide the mix between the two ramekins and bake for 28 to 33 minutes, or until the top becomes a deep golden brown and the mix is baked through.

5 Allow to cool on the counter for at least 10 minutes, then serve with serving options of your choice!

NEW YORK–STYLE BAGELS

These bagels are fun to make and will make you feel like you're in a busy New York City diner.

....

PREP TIME: 30 MINUTES (PLUS 1 HOUR RISING TIME)
COOK TIME: 40 MINUTES
YIELD: 6 LARGE BAGELS

....

INGREDIENTS

½ cup (125ml) plus 2 to 3 tbsp nondairy milk, divided

2 tbsp plus 1 tsp sugar

½ cup (125ml) water

2 tsp dry active yeast

3¼ cups (390g) all-purpose flour or bread flour, plus more for work surface

2½ tbsp (37g) vital wheat gluten (or substitute with flour)

2 tsp salt

2 to 4 tsp vegetable oil, divided

optional:

1 to 2 tbsp everything bagel seasoning (**page 50**)

1 In a small saucepan over medium-high, add ½ cup milk and the sugar. Cook until the sugar completely dissolves, stirring occasionally. Be sure not to let it reach a boil.

2 Pour the milk into a large bowl and add the water. At this stage, it should be moderately warm, at about 104°F (40°C).

3 Sprinkle the yeast over top and let sit, in a warm protected spot, for 10 minutes or until frothy.

4 Meanwhile, add the flour, vital wheat gluten, and salt to a medium bowl and mix well.

5 Add the flour mix to the milk mixture. Using a wooden spoon, mix until roughly combined. Transfer to a lightly floured work surface. Drizzle 1 to 2 teaspoons of vegetable oil over top and knead the dough with your hands for 8 to 10 minutes. The goal is to get the dough into a smooth, slightly sticky ball.

6 Use the remaining oil to coat a medium bowl (you can reuse the one you mixed the dry ingredients in). Place the ball of dough in the bowl. Cover with a clean dish towel and place it somewhere warm for 1 hour. While the dough rises, line a baking sheet with parchment paper.

7 Once the dough has risen, knead it for another minute.

8 Cut the dough into 6 equal-size pieces. Each one should weigh around 4 ounces (115g).

9 To shape each bagel, mold a piece of dough into a ball. Poke a hole into the center of the ball using your thumb. Widen the hole further by adding your other thumb and move the dough in your hands in a clockwise or counterclockwise motion to stretch the dough into bagel shape (see photos 1 to 4). The hole in the center should be about an inch, as it will shrink by the time the bagels are done. Place each shaped bagel onto the parchment paper and let rest for 10 to 15 minutes.

10 Meanwhile, bring a medium pot of water to a boil and preheat the oven to 375°F (190°C).

11 Add each bagel to the boiling water, letting it float to the top. Boil each bagel for 1 to 2 minutes, then flip it and boil for another 1 to 2 minutes on the other side. Cook up to 3 bagels at a time, depending on the size of your pot. Do not let the bagels touch as they boil or they will stick together.

12 Carefully shake off any excess water before placing the bagels back on the baking sheet, leaving space between each bagel. Brush the bagels with the remaining milk and sprinkle with everything bagel seasoning, if desired. Bake for 22 to 25 minutes, or until golden brown. Serve immediately.

MISO EGGPLANT WRAPS

PREP TIME: 15 MINUTES
COOK TIME: 25 MINUTES
YIELD: 3 WRAPS

INGREDIENTS

1 small to medium eggplant

2 tsp vegetable oil

2 tsp miso paste

2 tsp soy sauce

1 tsp maple syrup

3 (10-in/25-cm) tortillas of choice

1 avocado

1 lime

3 handfuls of arugula or baby spinach

1 bell pepper, thinly sliced

for the sauce:

3 tbsp plain soy yogurt

1 tbsp vegan mayonnaise

2 tsp white wine vinegar

pinch of salt

other spices of choice

So much umami going on in these wraps!

1 Preheat the oven to 400°F (200°C). Cut the eggplant lengthwise into 6 slices. Lay them out on a baking sheet lined with parchment paper.

2 In a small bowl, combine the vegetable oil, miso paste, soy sauce, and maple syrup into a paste.

3 Spread the paste evenly onto the eggplant slices. Bake for 20 to 25 minutes.

4 Meanwhile, to prepare the sauce, in a small bowl combine the yogurt, mayonnaise, vinegar, salt, and other spices of choice.

5 Assemble the wraps. Apply an equal amount of mashed avocado to the center of a tortilla. Squeeze over some lime juice, add a handful of greens, some bell pepper slices, and two roasted eggplant slices. Lastly, drizzle an equal portion of sauce over top.

6 Roll it up! Fold the end closest to you over the filling and pull the filling back toward you. Fold the left and right sides inward and then continue rolling it away from you. Repeat steps 5 and 6 until all wraps have been rolled.

7 Heat a nonstick skillet on medium-high. Place the rolled wraps, open side facing down, into the skillet and let them crisp up for 1 to 2 minutes on each side. Enjoy!

LENTIL KIMCHI BOWL

PREP TIME: 15 MINUTES (PLUS
    OPTIONAL MARINATING TIME)
COOK TIME: 5 MINUTES
YIELD: 2 SERVINGS

INGREDIENTS

1 (14oz/400g) can brown
    lentils, rinsed and drained

½ cucumber, cut into chunks

1 small carrot, cut into
    ribbons with a vegetable
    peeler

1 baby romaine lettuce heart,
    cut into chunks

1 cooked beet, cut into
    chunks

¼ cup (20g) sprouts

½ tbsp to 1 tbsp vegetable oil

for the marinade:

1½ tbsp soy sauce

1 tsp vegetable oil

1 tbsp rice vinegar

1 tbsp maple syrup

⅓ cup (50g) vegan kimchi,
    plus more for serving

for the peanut sauce:

¼ cup (60g) natural runny
    peanut or almond butter

1½ tbsp soy sauce

2 tbsp rice vinegar

2 tsp maple or rice syrup

2 tbsp warm water, more if
    needed

for serving:

2 pita breads

2 tsp sesame seeds

There's peanut sauce in this. That should be enough to sell you on this recipe, right?

1   Combine all ingredients for the marinade in a medium bowl.

2   Add the lentils to the marinade and mix well. Set aside. You can also marinate the lentils ahead of time for up to 24 hours in the fridge.

3   Divide the vegetables between two bowls.

4   Heat the vegetable oil in a medium nonstick pan on medium-high. Add the lentils, including all the marinade. Let cook for 4 to 5 minutes, stirring frequently.

5   Toast the pita bread. Meanwhile, combine all the ingredients for the peanut sauce and mix well. Adjust consistency with more water, if needed.

6   Divide the sautéed lentils between the two bowls and cover with the peanut sauce. Finish everything off with sesame seeds, additional kimchi, and the pita bread. Enjoy!

SNACKS

BBQ HUMMUS & TOFU BITES

PREP TIME: 5 MINUTES
COOK TIME: 25 MINUTES
YIELD: 10 TO 12 NUGGETS

INGREDIENTS

7oz (200g) firm plain tofu

1 tbsp nutritional yeast

1 tbsp white wine vinegar or
  lemon juice

2 tbsp vegan barbecue sauce

2 tbsp plain hummus

½ tsp smoked paprika

½ tsp salt

1 tbsp cornstarch

These nuggets are super unique in both taste and texture. Try them yourself to find out what these are all about!

1 Preheat the oven to 350°F (180°C) and line a baking sheet with parchment paper.

2 Add the tofu, nutritional yeast, vinegar, barbecue sauce, hummus, paprika, salt, and cornstarch to a food processor and blend on high until smooth. Be sure to pause from time to time to scrape down the excess mixture on the sides to ensure a full blend.

3 Using a tablespoon, spoon the mixture onto the baking sheet in spaced out dollops (see photo 1). Each heaping tablespoon of mixture should become one nugget. No need to shape the nuggets, although you can smooth out the top of each dollop with wet fingers if you'd like smoother looking nuggets (see photo 2).

4 Bake these for 22 to 25 minutes, or until golden brown. Serve immediately. Enjoy!

Tip: I love serving these with some cucumber, and dipped into some spicy vegan mayo! For the mayo, I simply combine 1 tablespoon of vegan mayonnaise and 1 teaspoon of my favorite hot sauce.

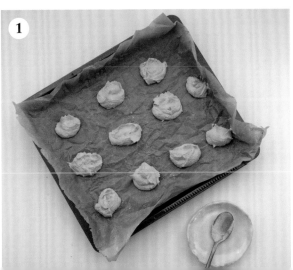

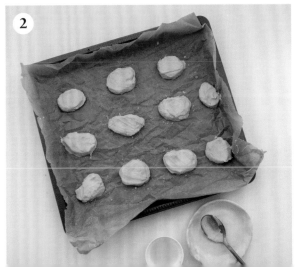

MOST AMAZING TAHINI DRESSING

PREP TIME: 6 MINUTES
COOK TIME: 30 MINUTES
YIELD: 2 TO 4 SERVINGS

INGREDIENTS

4 to 6 cloves garlic, unpeeled

4½ tbsp white tahini

2½ tbsp fresh lemon juice

2 tbsp soy sauce

1½ tbsp maple syrup

⅓ cup (80ml) orange juice, plus more if needed

The title says it all. Even if you're not the biggest fan of tahini, I urge you to try this sauce.

1 Preheat the oven to 350°F (180°C) and line a baking sheet with parchment paper.

2 Place the unpeeled garlic cloves on the parchment paper. Roast for 25 to 30 minutes, or until the garlic turns a deep golden brown.*

3 Allow the roasted garlic to cool down enough to be peeled. While it's cooling down, add the remaining ingredients to a blender. Peel the garlic cloves and add them to the blender as well. Blend everything until smooth, using a tamper if necessary. For a thinner consistency, add some water or more orange juice. Enjoy!

Tip: Where to use this sauce? Dip with sweet potato fries, raw vegetable sticks, or **Crispy Tofu Bites (page 76)**. Add to your sandwich, on top of your bowls, or over the **Falafel Crumble Tacos (page 61)**.

Note:

*In order to get some more use out of your oven, I recommend placing some lightly oiled vegetables next to the roasting garlic, which cook for the same amount of time. I like to use bell peppers, zucchini slices, and sweet potato chunks, but any will do.

VEGAN TZATZIKI

PREP TIME: 10 MINUTES
COOK TIME: 30 MINUTES
YIELD: 2 TO 3 SERVINGS

INGREDIENTS

½ cup (75g) cashews

⅓ medium cucumber

pinch of salt (plus more to taste)

1 cup (250g) thick plain soy yogurt

2 cloves garlic, peeled

2 tsp white wine vinegar or lemon juice

2 tsp olive oil

ground black pepper, to taste

Tzatziki was one of my favorite foods as a kid. This one comes incredibly close to the original. The cashews add a richness plain soy yogurt just can't provide on its own.

1 Boil the cashews in a small pot for 30 minutes.

2 Slice the cucumber in half lengthwise. Using a teaspoon, scoop out the seeds and discard them (or snack on them). Using a cheese grater, grate each half of the cucumber. Add a generous pinch of salt to the grated cucumber and set aside.

3 Drain the cashews and give them a quick rinse with cold water. Add the nuts to a food processor together with the yogurt, garlic, vinegar, and oil. Blend until smooth, scraping down the sides a few times, as needed.

4 Over a mesh strainer, squeeze out the salted cucumber with your hands, removing as much of the water as you can. Add the squeezed out cucumber to the blended cashew mix.

5 Season with salt and black pepper to taste. Serve with some pita bread, crackers, or vegetable sticks. Store in the fridge for up to three days.

Tip: This is really good together with the **Quinoa Lentil Bars (page 136)** or the **Pink Bulgur Bowl (page 76)**!

GARDEN VEGGIE JALAPEÑO DIP

PREP TIME: 10 MINUTES
COOK TIME: 45 MINUTES
YIELD: 6 SERVINGS

This is simply a delicious and reliable dip—perfect for meal prepping or sharing with friends and family!

INGREDIENTS

for the roasted vegetables:

1 medium onion, cut into rough chunks

1 bell pepper, cut into ½-inch (1¼-cm) strips

3 medium tomatoes, cut into ½-inch (1¼-cm) slices

2 to 3 cloves garlic, unpeeled

1 to 2 tbsp vegetable oil

salt, to taste

ground black pepper, to taste

for the dip:

1 cup (135g) sunflower seeds

2 tbsp vegetable oil

¼ cup (60ml) unsweetened nondairy milk

1 tbsp nutritional yeast

1 tbsp white wine vinegar or lemon juice

1 tbsp soy sauce

1 tbsp tomato paste

salt, to taste

ground black pepper, to taste

1 pickled jalapeño, cut into slices, or more to taste

1 Preheat the oven to 400°F (200°C) and line a baking sheet with parchment paper.

2 Transfer the onion, bell pepper, tomato, and garlic to the sheet and drizzle vegetable oil over top. Toss until everything is evenly coated in oil. Then arrange the veggies in one even layer and season with salt and black pepper. Bake for 40 to 45 minutes.

3 Meanwhile, in a small to medium pot of water, boil the sunflower seeds for 30 minutes. Drain the seeds when finished.

4 When the vegetables have cooled sufficiently for handling, pick out the garlic cloves and peel them.

5 Add the roasted garlic to a high speed blender along with all the other roasted vegetables, the boiled sunflower seeds, oil, milk, yeast, vinegar, soy sauce, tomato paste, and jalapeno slices. Blend until smooth, pushing down the ingredients with a tamper as you blend. Once smooth, taste and season with salt and black pepper.

6 Serve immediately or store in an airtight container in the fridge for up to 3 days. This dip can also be used as a spread for toast, or as a base for salad dressings and pasta sauces. There are so many options!

Tip: Make some **Baked Paprika Tortilla Chips (page 118)** to enjoy with this dip!

BAKED PAPRIKA TORTILLA CHIPS

PREP TIME: 4 MINUTES
COOK TIME: 6 TO 10 MINUTES
YIELD: 2 TO 3 SERVINGS

A clever way of using up leftover tortillas is to turn them into chips! Try my suggested paprika flavoring or get creative and see what you can come up with spice-wise.

INGREDIENTS

5 to 6 medium (10in/25cm) tortillas

1 tbsp nutritional yeast

¼ tsp salt

½ tsp smoked paprika

½ tsp sweet or spicy paprika

¼ tsp garlic powder

1 tbsp vegetable oil

1 Preheat the oven to 375°F (190°C). Line a baking sheet with parchment paper.

2 Stack the tortillas on top of each other and cut them into 6 to 8 triangles. Transfer them to a large mixing bowl.

3 Add the yeast, salt, spices, and oil to the bowl as well and gently combine everything by hand until the tortillas are evenly coated.

4 Lay the tortillas out on your baking sheet in one even layer. If the sheet seems too crowded, consider baking in two batches.

5 Bake the chips for 6 to 8 minutes, or until golden brown and slightly darkened along the edges. Keep a close watch, as they can burn quickly. If using a light-colored baking sheet, you may need to bake for up to 10 minutes.

6 Allow the chips to cool and crisp up for a few minutes before serving!

Tip: I recommend serving these chips with some **Garden Veggie Jalapeño Dip (page 117)**!

ORANGE BOK CHOY

PREP TIME: 10 MIN
COOK TIME: 10 MIN
YIELD: 2 SERVINGS

INGREDIENTS

1 tbsp vegetable oil

1lb (500g) bok choy, trimmed* and quartered**

for the sauce:

4 cloves garlic, minced

1-inch piece of ginger, peeled and minced

pinch of chili flakes, or to taste

1 to 2 tsp sesame seeds

1½ tbsp soy sauce

2 tsp maple syrup

zest of ½ an orange

1 tbsp rice vinegar

¼ cup (60ml) orange juice

pinch of salt

pinch of ground black pepper

This is a lovely side dish best served paired with crispy tofu and rice.

1   In a small bowl combine all the ingredients for the sauce.

2   Heat the vegetable oil in a large skillet on medium-high. Once hot, carefully add the bok choy pieces to the pan in one even layer using tongs. Do not move the pieces around. Allow them to get some color for about 1 to 2 minutes. Turn the bok choy and let the other sides brown as well for 1 to 2 minutes each.

3   Reduce heat to medium and add the orange mixture to the pan. Allow to simmer for 2 to 3 minutes. Serve and enjoy! If you would like to make a whole meal out of this, plate the bok choy next to some rice and tofu.

Notes:

*Cut off the outermost part of the stem. Don't cut off too much, or it will fall apart. If this happens, this recipe still works with chopped bok choy. It just won't look as pretty!

**If using baby bok choy, only cut them in half.

CHICKPEA GRANOLA

PREP TIME: 10 MINUTES
COOK TIME: 30 MINUTES
YIELD: 3 SERVINGS, DEPENDING ON USE

This salty mix of roasted chickpeas, toasted oats, nuts, and seeds is insanely delicious. Use it atop salads, toast, unsweetened yogurt, or simply by the handful.

INGREDIENTS

for the chickpeas:

1 cup (170g) chickpeas, drained and rinsed

1 tbsp olive oil

¼ tsp paprika

¼ tsp garlic powder

¼ tsp ground turmeric

¼ tsp onion powder

pinch of salt

1 tbsp nutritional yeast

for the seed mix:

1 tbsp olive oil

2 tbsp hemp seeds

⅓ cup (45g) sunflower seeds

⅓ cup (45g) peanuts, walnuts, or almonds

⅓ cup (30g) old-fashioned oats

pinch of salt

1 Preheat the oven to 415°F (210°C) and line a baking sheet with parchment paper (or aluminum foil for extra crispiness).

2 Add the chickpeas to the baking sheet. Drizzle the olive oil overtop. Add the paprika, garlic powder, turmeric, onion powder, salt, and nutritional yeast. Mix with your hands, ensuring the chickpeas are evenly coated.

3 Bake the chickpeas in a single layer for about 25 minutes, or until deep golden brown.

4 About 7 minutes before the chickpeas are done, start the seed mix. Heat the olive oil in a medium skilled on medium. Add the seeds, nuts, oats, and salt. Mix well. Let this toast for 3 to 5 minutes, mixing occasionally, until golden brown and fragrant.

5 Remove the chickpeas from the oven and add the contents of the skillet to the baking sheet. Let this sit for at least 10 minutes, then serve. Snack on this as is or add to a salad or bowl for some added crunch! Keep stored in an airtight container for up to 3 days.

Tip: You can even serve this like you would regular granola! Add a few drops of white wine vinegar or lemon or lime juice to a bowl of unsweetened plain soy yogurt and mix well. Next, add some of the granola, plus some chopped parsley, cucumber chunks, and a sprinkle of sumac, cumin, or paprika.

5-MINUTE CUCUMBER SALAD

PREP TIME: 3 MINUTES
COOK TIME: 2 MINUTES
YIELD: 1 TO 2 SERVINGS

Inspired by Japanese Sunomono, this cucumber salad checks all the boxes. It's quick to make, good for you, and so, so delicious!

INGREDIENTS

1 medium cucumber

1 to 2 tsp sesame seeds

2 tbsp rice vinegar

¼ tsp chili flakes

2 tsp rice, maple, or agave syrup

2 tsp soy sauce

salt, to taste

1 Peel the cucumber into ribbons using a vegetable peeler.

2 Add the sesame seeds to a small, dry skillet on medium. Stir for 2 minutes until the seeds are fragrant and golden brown.

3 Transfer the roasted sesame seeds to a small bowl along with the vinegar, chili flakes, syrup, and soy sauce. Mix well. Add the cucumber and mix again. Lastly, add salt, to taste.

APPLE PIE ENERGY BITES

PREP TIME: 10 MIN
COOK TIME: NONE
YIELD: 10 TO 12 BITES

INGREDIENTS

1 cup (150g) soft pitted dates

⅔ cup (70g) quick-cooking oats

pinch of salt

½ tsp vanilla extract

½ tsp cinnamon

3 tbsp ground flax seeds

3 tbsp unsweetened applesauce

I also refer to these as sweet and salty spiced bites of pure heaven.

1   Add the dates, oats, generous pinch of salt, vanilla, cinnamon, flax seeds, and applesauce to a food processor and blend for a few minutes, scraping down the sides as needed until you have a malleable mixture. It is okay if the mixture is a bit chunky.

2   Roll this mixture into 10 to 12 bite-size balls. These taste best once they've sat in the fridge for a bit. So refrigerate for at least 30 minutes and then serve! Store in an airtight container in the fridge for up to 3 days, or in the freezer for a few weeks.

SWEET POTATO CHOCOLATE OAT BARS

PREP TIME: 15 MINUTES
COOK TIME: 50 MINUTES
YIELD: 4 SERVINGS

INGREDIENTS

1 medium (14oz/400g) sweet
   potato

2 cups (180g) quick-cooking
   oats

1 tbsp ground flax seeds

3 tbsp sugar

½ tsp salt

½ tsp cinnamon

½ tsp baking powder

2 tbsp vegetable oil

⅓ cup (40g) pecans or
   walnuts, chopped

¼ cup (45g) vegan dark
   chocolate, broken into
   chunks

These are incredibly cozy and nutritious oat bars that make for a great snack any time of day.

1 Bring a medium pot of water to a boil. Meanwhile, peel the sweet potato and cut it into 2-inch (5-cm) chunks. Add them to the water and let boil for about 10 minutes, or until tender. Drain.

2 Preheat the oven to 350°F (180°C) and line an 8x8-in baking dish (20x20-cm) with wet parchment paper (see p.23). Make sure you leave parchment paper hanging over the sides of the pan to make it easier to lift out later.

3 Add the oats, flax seeds, sugar, salt, cinnamon, and baking powder to a food processor. Blend until fine and powdery.

4 Next, add the drained sweet potato chunks and vegetable oil and blend again.

5 Using a rubber spatula, press the slightly sticky mixture into the baking dish. Sprinkle over the chopped nuts, pressing them into the batter. Bake for 35 to 42 minutes. Set aside to cool completely.

6 Melt the chocolate.* Drizzle the melted chocolate over the bake. Let the chocolate set before lifting from the pan and slicing into bars. Store in an airtight container in the fridge for up to 4 days.

Notes:

*Feel free to use whatever melting method works best for you. For this recipe, I use the following: Melt the chocolate in the oven in a medium oven proof bowl at 300.F (150.C) for 5 minutes. Carefully remove the bowl and let sit for 5 minutes before mixing the chocolate until fully melted.

PEANUT BUTTER PROTEIN BARS

PREP TIME: 18 MINUTES
COOK TIME: 5 MINUTES (PLUS 30
    MINUTES COOL TIME)
YIELD: 6 BARS

INGREDIENTS

½ (45g) cup oats

¼ cup plus 1 tbsp (35g) vegan
vanilla protein powder (or
substitute with more oats)

pinch of salt

1 tbsp flax meal (golden flax
meal preferred)

½ cup (120g) natural peanut
butter

¼ cup (60g) unsweetened
applesauce

½ tsp vanilla extract

3 tbsp rice, maple, agave, or
date syrup

1 to 2 tbsp nondairy milk, if
needed

½ cup (90g) dark chocolate

1 tsp coconut oil (optional)

Never spend money on overpriced protein bars again!

1   Line a baking sheet with parchment paper.

2   In a food processor, add the oats, protein powder, salt, and
flax meal. Blend until fine and powdery.

3   Add the peanut butter, applesauce, vanilla, and syrup. Blend
again. If the mixture feels a bit dry, add 1 to 2 tablespoons of
nondairy milk. The mixed dough should be malleable and
easy to work with.

4   Now shape the mixture into 6 bars (each one weighing about
1.75oz/50g) and let them rest on the baking sheet. I
recommend transferring the sheet to the fridge or freezer
while you're melting the chocolate. However, this is optional.

5   Melt the chocolate.* Add the coconut oil to the melted
chocolate. This will add some shine to the bars.

6   One at a time, dip the bars into the chocolate. Cover each side
evenly. Allow any excess chocolate to drip down into the bowl
before placing the coated bar back onto the baking sheet. I
prefer to balance each bar on two forks to get an even coat of
chocolate. Repeat with the remaining bars.

7   Allow the chocolate to harden before serving. Simply put
them in the fridge or freezer for 15 to 30 minutes. Store in the
fridge for up to 5 days or in the freezer for up to 3 weeks.

Note:

*Feel free to use whatever melting method works best for you. For this recipe,
I use the following: Melt the chocolate in the oven in a medium oven proof
bowl at 300.F (150.C) for 5 minutes. Carefully remove the bowl and let sit for
5 minutes before mixing the chocolate until fully melted.

ALMOND BUTTER PROTEIN BITES

PREP TIME: 15 MINUTES
COOK TIME: 5 MINUTES (PLUS 30
   MINUTES COOL TIME)
YIELD: 5 TO 6 BARS

INGREDIENTS

½ cup (45g) quick-cooking
   oats

2 tbsp hemp seed flour or 2½
   tbsp hulled hemp seeds

3 tbsp pumpkin seeds

2 tbsp sunflower seeds

2 tbsp ground flax seeds

1½ tbsp unsweetened cocoa
   powder

pinch of salt

¼ tsp cinnamon or
   gingerbread spice

½ cup (120g) almond butter

¼ cup (60g) unsweetened
   applesauce

½ tsp vanilla extract

2½ tbsp rice, maple, agave, or
   date syrup

½ cup plus 1 tbsp (100g)
   dark chocolate

The love child of a protein bar and a German gingerbread cookie.

1 Line a baking sheet with parchment paper.

2 Add the oats, hemp, pumpkin seeds, sunflower seeds, flax seeds, cocoa powder, salt, and cinnamon to a food processor and blend until fine and powdery.

3 Next, add the almond butter, applesauce, vanilla, and syrup and blend until a dough forms.

4 Shape the dough into 5 to 6 equal-size bars and let them rest on the baking sheet. I recommend transferring the sheet to the fridge or freezer while you're melting the chocolate, but that's optional.

5 Melt the chocolate.*

6 One at a time, dip the bars into the chocolate. Cover each side evenly. Allow any excess chocolate to drip down into the bowl before placing the coated bar back onto the baking sheet. I prefer to balance each bar on two forks to get an even coat of chocolate. Repeat with the remaining bars.

7 Allow the chocolate to harden before serving. Simply put them in the fridge or freezer for 15 to 30 minutes. Store in the fridge of up to 5 days or in the freezer for up to 3 weeks.

Note:

*Feel free to use whatever melting method works best for you. For this recipe, I use the following: Melt the chocolate in the oven in a medium oven proof bowl at 300.F (150.C) for 5 minutes. Carefully remove the bowl and let sit for 5 minutes before mixing the chocolate until fully melted.

MINTY ICED CHOCOLATE

PREP TIME: 5 MINUTES
COOK TIME: 5 MINUTES (PLUS 15 TO
    20 MINUTES COOLING TIME)
YIELD: 1 SERVING

Refreshing and cozy at the same time, this drink uses cornstarch to give you a luxurious, creamy hot chocolate experience, but in an iced, summery form.

INGREDIENTS

½ tsp cornstarch

2 to 3 tsp unsweetened cocoa
    powder, to taste

pinch of salt

1 cup (250ml) nondairy milk,
    divided

2 tsp preferred sweetener

1 peppermint tea bag

8 to 10 ice cubes, divided

1 In a small saucepan, whisk together the cornstarch, cocoa powder, salt, and ¼ cup (60ml) of the milk until smooth.

2 Add the remaining milk and the sweetener. Bring to a quick boil, whisking throughout. Let simmer for 30 seconds to 1 minute, whisking every once in a while, before removing from the heat. Add the tea bag. Let steep and cool for 7 to 10 minutes. Stir every few minutes to prevent a layer from forming on the surface.

3 Remove the tea bag. Add 4 ice cubes to a jar that is capable of holding at least 1 cup (250ml) of liquid. Pour in the minty chocolate. Seal the jar with a lid and shake until the cocoa has cooled down completely. Add the remaining ice cubes to the jar and serve. Alternatively, divide and serve 2 smaller portions.

QUINOA LENTIL BARS

PREP TIME: 10 MINUTES
COOK TIME: 70 MINUTES
YIELD: 4 TO 6 SERVINGS

INGREDIENTS

½ cup (85g) rinsed quinoa

½ cup (95g) black lentils

2⅔ cups (660ml) water, divided; plus more if needed

1 tbsp vegetable oil, for frying

1 onion, chopped

3.5oz (100g) smoked tofu, cut into cubes

1 to 2 cloves garlic, minced

1½ cups (135g) quick-cooking oats

1¼ tsp salt

½ cup (60g) white spelt flour or all-purpose flour

pinch of ground black pepper

¼ tsp cumin

½ tsp paprika

pinch of ground turmeric

1 tbsp white wine vinegar

1 tbsp soy sauce

serving options:

Vegan Tzatziki (page 114)

cucumber slices

hummus

vegan cream cheese

Someone once told me these bars have a "very old-school, 1970s hippie health food vibe." Need I say more?

1 To a medium or large pot, add the quinoa, black lentils, and 2 cups (500ml) of the water. Bring to a boil and cover with a lid.* Reduce heat to medium and simmer 15 to 20 minutes, or until the quinoa and lentils are cooked through and nearly all water has been absorbed.**

2 Meanwhile, heat the vegetable oil in a nonstick skillet on medium. Add the onion and tofu, and fry for approximately 6 minutes. Add the garlic and let cook for an additional 2 to 3 minutes. Set aside.

3 Preheat the oven to 350ºF (180ºC) and line an 8- or 9-inch (20- or 23-cm) brownie pan or casserole dish with wet parchment paper (see p.23). Make sure you leave parchment paper hanging over the sides of the pan to make it easier to lift out later.

4 Add the oats and the remaining ⅔ cup (160ml) of water to the lentils and quinoa. Mix well. Let cook for another 3 to 5 minutes, stirring frequently.

5 Add the tofu micture to the pot and mix. Then add the salt, flour, spices, vinegar, and soy sauce. Mix well. If it is too thick, add another ¼ cup (60ml) of water.

6 Add the mixture to the baking dish and, using a rubber spatula, gently pat it into an even layer.

7 Bake for 50 minutes until firm and crispy around the edges. Let cool for at least 20 minutes before lifting from the pan, slicing, and serving. The slices can be stored in an airtight container in the freezer for up to three weeks. Serve with the optional toppings, or get creative and add your own!

Notes:

*I recommend using a lid with a small hole for the steam to escape.

**Keep an eye on the pot. Toward the beginning of the cooking process, the water might start to overflow. Simply lift the lid for a few seconds when you feel like this is about to happen. Repeat as needed.

ALMOND CHOCOLATE CRUMBLES

PREP TIME: 5 MINUTES
COOK TIME: 10 MINUTES
YIELD: 4 SERVINGS

This nutty brownie mixture is the perfect topping for yogurt or smoothie bowls.

INGREDIENTS

⅔ cup (100g) pitted dates

½ cup (50g) almonds

½ cup (45g) oats

1 tbsp ground flax seeds

pinch of salt

2½ tbsp unsweetened cocoa powder

1 to 2 tbsp nondairy milk, if needed

1   Preheat the oven to 350°F (180°C) and line a baking sheet with parchment paper.

2   Cover the dates with hot water and let them soak for 10 to 15 minutes, then drain them.

3   Meanwhile, place the almonds in a single layer on the baking sheet and let them bake for 8 minutes.

4   To a food processor, add the drained dates, roasted almonds, oats, flax seeds, salt, and cocoa powder. Blend until it resembles chunky granola. If it's too dry, add 1 tablespoon of nondairy milk at a time as you blend.

5   Serve as is, as a snack. Alternatively, this makes for a great topping for a bowl of yogurt and berries, a smoothie bowl, or vegan ice cream! You can even serve it as cereal with nondairy milk. Store in an airtight container in the fridge for up to 4 days.

CHOCOLATE HUMMUS

PREP TIME: 8 MINUTES
COOK TIME: NONE
YIELD: 2 SERVINGS

INGREDIENTS

1 (14oz/400g) can white beans, drained and rinsed

3 tbsp quick-cooking oats

3 tbsp unsweetened cocoa powder

½ tsp salt

1 tsp vanilla extract

2½ tbsp liquid sweetener

2½ tbsp sugar

2½ tbsp melted vegan butter or melted coconut oil

1½ tbsp nondairy milk, more if needed

If you've never had chocolate hummus, here's your sign to try it! My recipe uses white beans instead of chickpeas, since white beans have a subtler flavor. So, all you're tasting is rich and creamy chocolate goodness.

1   Place all ingredients in a food processor. Blend until completely smooth, pushing down the ingredients if the food processor stops blending. Adjust the consistency with more milk, if needed.

2   Serve with anything from rice cakes to cookies to berries. Enjoy!

ALMOND CHOCOLATE SAUCE

PREP TIME: 3 MINUTES
COOK TIME: NONE
YIELD: 1 SERVING

INGREDIENTS

1 tbsp almond butter

2 tsp unsweetened cocoa powder

1½ tsp maple syrup or liquid sweetener

1 to 2 tbsp nondairy milk, more if needed

pinch of salt

This sauce is perfect on anything sweet. Eat it with strawberries, ice cream, yogurt, cake, or straight with a spoon.

1 In a small bowl, combine all the ingredients. Mix well. Adjust the consistency with more milk, as needed.

2 Serve immediately over some yogurt, porridge, or a smoothie bowl! This also works as a dip.

Tip: I recommend serving this together with my delicious **Pretzel Baked Cheesecake (page 201).**

PEANUT MILK

PREP TIME: 5 MINUTES
COOK TIME: NONE
YIELD: CLOSE TO 2 CUPS (ABOUT
    450ML)

INGREDIENTS

2 to 3 tbsp natural peanut
    butter

pinch of salt

1½ cups (375ml) water

4 to 6 ice cubes

1 to 2 tsp liquid sweetener
    (optional)

A life saver for when you've run out of milk, this peanut-y drink is perfect for cereal and museli, or when you have cookies to dunk! You can also make this with almond, cashew, or hazelnut butter!

1 Add all the ingredients to a blender and blend until smooth.

2 Serve immediately or store in the fridge for up to 3 days. Shake or stir before serving.

Tip: This milk is great on its own, in cereal and museli, or for baking!

PUMPKIN JUICE

PREP TIME: 7 MINUTES (PLUS 15
MINUTES SOAKING TIME)
COOK TIME: 5 MINUTES (45
MINUTES IF ROASTING PUMPKIN)
YIELD: 2 TO 3 SERVINGS

INGREDIENTS

1 small hokkaido pumpkin
or ½ cup plus 1 tbsp
(100g) roasted or canned
pumpkin

1 tbsp fresh lemon juice

½ tsp vanilla extract

¼ tsp cinnamon

¼ tsp pumpkin pie spice

3 to 5 soft pitted dates*

2 cups (500ml) apple juice

1 cup (250ml) water

ice cubes, for serving

If Halloween were a drink, this would be it. Serve this cozy pumpkin punch either hot or iced.

1 If roasting the pumpkin, preheat the oven to 375°F (190°C) and line a baking sheet with parchment paper. Cut the pumpkin in half, removing the seeds and placing the halves cut side down on the baking sheet. Roast for about 45 minutes. Let cool and remove the skin.

2 Measure out the roasted pumpkin. Add the pumpkin and remaining ingredients to a blender and blend until smooth.

3 Serve iced or hot. To serve hot, heat in a small pot on medium-high for 2 to 3 minutes. Divide between 2 to 3 glasses or cups. Enjoy!

Notes:

*If your dates are on the dry side, place them in a bowl, pour hot water over top of them, and let them soak for 10 to 15 minutes. Drain the water before adding the dates to the blender.

GO-TO VEGAN SNACK IDEAS

Sometimes you really just want something simple. Something that only takes a few moments to put together—the quicker the better. Here's a list of some super simple snack ideas I love. Feel free to get creative with these and swap out similar ingredients that you have on hand. Also, don't be scared to play around with the measurements and ratios. I usually eyeball most things here anyway. Enjoy!

SWEET

1   Dip dried apricots in peanut butter, almond butter, or cashew butter.

2   Add vegan cream cheese, 2 tablespoons of warmed frozen cherries, and a drizzle of maple syrup to some whole wheat toast.

3   Add a squeeze of lemon juice, a sprinkle of cinnamon, and a sprinkle of salt to apple slices.

4   Fill some dates with almond butter and top with shredded coconut and a sprinkle of salt.

5   In a mug, whisk together 1 to 2 teaspoons of unsweetened cocoa powder, 1 to 2 teaspoons of sweetener, and ¼ cup (60ml) hot water. Add 1 chai tea bag and ¾ cup (180ml) warm nondairy milk and steep for 5 minutes before serving.

6   Sprinkle a light dusting of cocoa powder on orange or mandarin slices and serve.

7   Mix 1 tablespoon of natural peanut butter with a sprinkle of salt and a sprinkle of cocoa nibs. Serve with banana slices or as is with a spoon.

8   Squeeze lemon or lime juice on frozen grapes. Wait 2 minutes, then serve.

9   Add fresh berries and a dusting of cocoa powder to thick plain vegan yogurt.

10 Iced vanilla matcha: Mix 1 teaspoon matcha powder with 3 tbsp hot water with a spoon or milk frother until smooth. Add 1 teaspoon of maple syrup, ½ tsp vanilla extract, and ¼ cup (60ml) cold water. Pour this mixture into a glass with ice cubes and a ½ cup (125ml) cold nondairy milk and stir.

SAVORY

1   Dip cucumber, bell peppers, or carrot sticks in 1 to 2 tablespoons of hummus mixed with ½ tsp gochujang or harissa.

2   Sprinkle nutritional yeast and fresh herbs over salted popcorn.

3   Add 1 heaping tablespoon of hummus plus 1 to 2 teaspoons of store-bought pesto on a rice cake with cherry tomatoes and hemp seeds.

4   Boil frozen edamame for 2 minutes. Sprinkle with salt and chili flakes before serving.

5   Spread avocado and balsamic glaze on crackers before serving.

6   Steam broccoli and serve with salt, a squeeze of lemon juice, a sprinkle of nutritional yeast, and a small drizzle of tahini.

7   Rub 1 piece of toast with ½ clove of garlic. Spread 1 teaspoon of vegan butter on the bread. Add ½ cooked beet, thinly sliced. Add a squeeze of lemon juice, a small drizzle of olive oil, and a sprinkle of salt.

8   Cut 1 medium carrot into ribbons using a vegetable peeler. Sauté in a little oil for 5 to 7 minutes on medium. Spread toast or rice cake with hummus. Add the carrots. Sprinkle salt overtop.

9   Warm 2 heaping tablespoons of vegan kimchi in a small pot for 2 minutes on medium. Spread peanut butter on a small or medium tortilla. Top with the warmed kimchi.

10 ½ cup (120g) black beans, 1 to 2 tablespoons of ketchup, and 1 teaspoon of sriracha on toast, crackers, rice cakes, or tostadas.

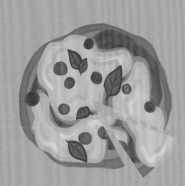

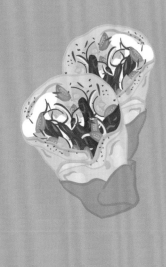

DINNER

ALMOND & MISO NOODLES

PREP TIME: 15 MINUTES
COOK TIME: 20 MINUTES
YIELD: 2 SERVINGS

Rice noodles covered in tangy almond sauce, roasted almond chunks, fried mushrooms, carrot noodles, and fresh lime juice—what's not to love?

INGREDIENTS

4½oz (130g) rice noodles

2½ tbsp rice vinegar

1 tbsp vegetable oil

1 onion, finely minced

¼ cup (35g) almonds, chopped

1 medium carrot, cut into ribbons using a vegetable peeler

4 to 5 cremini mushrooms, cut into small chunks

2 cloves garlic, minced

salt, to taste

juice of 1 lime

¼ cup (15g) cilantro, finely chopped

for the miso sauce:

1 tbsp nutritional yeast

1½ tbsp rice vinegar

2 tbsp soy sauce

1½ tbsp miso paste

1½ tbsp almond butter

2 tbsp brown sugar or maple syrup

pinch of mild chili flakes

½ cup (125ml) hot water, plus more if needed

1 To prepare the sauce, add the nutritional yeast, vinegar, soy sauce, miso paste, almond butter, sugar, and chili flakes in a medium bowl. Pour in the hot water. Using a whisk, mix thoroughly until smooth. Set aside.

2 Place the rice noodles in a large heatproof bowl and cover with boiling water. Add the rice vinegar to the bowl as well. Let this sit for 8 to 10 minutes, or until al dente. Drain.

3 Heat the vegetable oil in a large nonstick skillet on medium-high. Add the onion, almonds, carrot, and mushrooms. Let cook for about 5 minutes, stirring frequently. Reduce heat to medium-low. Add the garlic and a splash of water. Stir and cook for 3 to 4 minutes. Then, pour in the sauce.

4 Rinse the noodles and add them to the skillet as well, followed by the lime juice. Mix carefully, so as not to break the noodles. I recommend using wooden spoons to lift and fold the noodles. Lastly, add salt, to taste.

5 Divide the noodles between two bowls. Finish off with cilantro and consider adding lime wedges and sesame seeds. Enjoy!

GREEK-STYLE PITA SANDWICHES

PREP TIME: 25 MINUTES (PLUS
    MARINATING AND TZATZIKI PREP
    TIME)
COOK TIME: 10 MINUTES
YIELD: 2 SANDWICHES

INGREDIENTS

7oz (200g) oyster mushrooms

for the marinade:

2 tbsp olive oil

1 tbsp fresh lemon juice

¼ tsp dried oregano

¼ tsp onion powder

¼ tsp garlic powder

¼ tsp ground black pepper

pinch of ground cinnamon

pinch of ground nutmeg

1 tsp cornstarch

1 tsp soy sauce

for assembling the sandwiches:

1 medium red onion, sliced
    into thin rings

2 pita breads

4 tbsp **Vegan Tzatziki (page
    114)** or hummus

1 medium tomato, thinly
    sliced

¼ cucumber, cubed

¼ cup (15g) chopped parsley

a generous pinch of salt, for
    seasoning the mushrooms

Oyster mushrooms are an amazing meat substitute!

1   Cut the oyster mushrooms into strips. Place the strips into
    a large tupperware container and add all the ingredients for
    the marinade. Stir well. Seal the container and let the
    mushrooms marinate in the fridge for at least 1 hour. Do not
    let them marinate for more than 24 hours, though!

2   Heat a grill pan on high, or a skillet on medium-high. Once
    hot, add the marinated mushrooms. Fry the mushrooms for 5
    to 7 minutes, or until golden brown and slightly crispy along
    the edges. Once they're done, add a generous pinch of salt to
    them and stir well.

3   Meanwhile, soak the red onions in a small bowl of hot water
    for a few minutes to allow the flavor to mellow a bit. Toast
    your pita bread and spread with a layer of tzatziki. Next, add
    the tomato, onion, cucumber, parsley, mushrooms, and
    additional tzatziki. Enjoy!

PASTA À LA VINO

PREP TIME: 15 MINUTES
COOK TIME: 40 MINUTES
YIELD: 3 SERVINGS

A fancy twist on pasta with tomato sauce, this is perfect for a cute at-home date night!

INGREDIENTS

1 tbsp vegan butter

1 tbsp olive oil

1 medium yellow onion, minced

pinch of chili flakes

3 cloves garlic, minced

2 tbsp tomato paste/purée

1 tsp maple syrup or sugar

¾ cup (180ml) white wine

1 cup (250ml) crushed tomatoes (otherwise known as passata)

½ cup (125ml) vegetable broth or water, plus more if needed

3 cups (280g) short cut pasta (penne, rigatoni, etc.)

salt, to taste

ground black pepper, to taste

¼ cup (6g) chopped parsley or basil (optional)

vegan Parmesan (**page 187**), or other vegan Parmesan (optional)

for the cashew cream:

½ cup (70g) cashews

½ cup (125ml) nondairy milk

1 tbsp nutritional yeast

1 tbsp lemon juice

pinch of salt

1 Boil the cashews in a small pot for about 30 minutes.

2 Meanwhile, heat the butter and olive oil in a large saucepan on medium. Once hot, add the onion and cook for about 5 minutes until the onions appear translucent. Then, add the chili flakes and garlic and cook for another 2 minutes. Add the tomato paste and maple syrup and cook for another minute, stirring frequently.

3 Pour in the white wine. Turn the heat to medium-high and bring to a boil. Let boil for 2 minutes, then add the crushed tomatoes and vegetable broth and reduce the heat to medium. Let simmer for 15 to 20 minutes.

4 Meanwhile, drain the cashews. Using a blender or food processor, blend together the cashews, milk, yeast, lemon juice, and a pinch of salt until smooth. This can take up to 2 minutes. Set aside.

5 Bring a large pot of salted water to a boil. Cook the pasta until al dente, according to package instructions.

6 Reserve 2 tablespoons of the cashew cream, and add the rest to the tomato sauce. Mix and season to taste with salt and black pepper. If the sauce is too thick, add more water.

7 Add the cooked pasta to the sauce. Serve this with some fresh basil and vegan parmesan! Drizzle the reserved cashew cream over top right before serving.

BEST EVER COUSCOUS

PREP TIME: 20 MINUTES
COOK TIME: 40 MINUTES
YIELD: 4 SERVINGS

Here's a vegan version of a dish I grew up eating all the time. There is no better way of eating couscous in my humble opinion.

INGREDIENTS

3 or 4 tbsp olive oil, divided

1 large onion, diced small

1 carrot, diced small

¼ tsp salt, plus more to taste

3 cloves garlic, minced

1½ tbsp tomato paste/purée

1 tsp harissa paste, or to taste

¼ tsp ground black pepper

½ tsp cumin

½ tsp sweet paprika

¼ tsp ground turmeric

¼ tsp ground cinnamon

½ tsp ground coriander

½ tsp ground cardamom

1 tbsp cornstarch

1 (14oz/400g) can chickpeas, drained and rinsed

4 cups (1liter) vegetable broth

2 medium potatoes, peeled and cut into 1 to 2-inch (2.5 to 5-cm) chunks

1 tbsp maple syrup

1 cup (250ml) water

1 cup (180g) dried couscous

3 or 4 long red, green, or yellow bell peppers

½ cup (100g) fresh or frozen green beans, cut in half, ends removed

parsley, for serving

1 Heat 2 tablespoons olive oil in a large pot on medium Once hot, add the onion, carrot, and a pinch of salt. Let cook for about 6 minutes. Next, add the garlic and stir. Then, add both the tomato paste and harissa paste. Stir. Let cook for another 1 to 2 minutes. Add the spices and cook 1 to 2 minutes more.

2 Stir in the cornstarch. Add the chickpeas, vegetable broth, potatoes, and syrup. Turn the heat up to high and bring to a boil. Reduce heat to medium and simmer for 20 to 35 minutes, or until the potatoes are tender.

3 Meanwhile, in a medium pot, bring the water, ¼ teaspoon salt, and 1 to 2 tablespoons olive oil to a boil. As soon as it is boiling, stir in the couscous. Turn the heat off and let sit uncovered for about 10 minutes, or until the couscous is cooked through. Fluff with a fork.

4 Remove the cores from the bell peppers and cut them in half or quarters lengthwise, resulting in long slivers. Pat the peppers dry with a paper towel, to prevent oil splashes later. Heat the vegetable oil in a grill pan or skillet on medium-high. Once hot, carefully add the pepper slices. Cook them for 2 to 3 minutes until they are lightly charred on each side.

5 Add the green beans to the tomato sauce and simmer 3 to 5 minutes. Season the sauce with salt, to taste. I recommend using quite a bit.

6 Divide the couscous, sauce, and grilled peppers between four plates and top with parsley, if desired. Enjoy!

GO-TO CHICKPEA RED CURRY

PREP TIME: 10 MINUTES
COOK TIME: 12 MINUTES
YIELD: 2 TO 3 SERVINGS

This is a fantastic, low effort curry. Instead of rice, go for noodles to get to dinner even faster.

INGREDIENTS

1 bell pepper, cut into large, rough chunks

1 medium onion, cut into rough chunks

2 cloves garlic, peeled

1-inch (2.5-cm) piece of ginger, peeled

½ tsp chili flakes

¾ tsp curry powder

1 tbsp tomato paste/purée

1½ tbsp lemon or lime juice, plus more to taste

1 tsp agave or maple syrup

1 to 2 tsp coconut oil

1 tsp cornstarch

¼ cup (60ml) water

1 (14oz/400g) can chickpeas, drained and rinsed

1 (13.5oz/400ml) can coconut milk

handful of chopped fresh parsley or cilantro

salt, to taste

ground black pepper, to taste

3 to 4 servings of cooked rice

sprinkle of sesame seeds

1 Add the bell pepper, onion, garlic, ginger, chili flakes, curry powder, tomato paste, lemon juice, and syrup to a food processor. Blend for a few seconds until you have a chunky purée of sorts.

2 Heat the coconut oil in a medium skillet over medium. Pour in the contents of the food processor. Cook for 6 to 8 minutes, adding a splash of water or two as it cooks.

3 In a small glass or bowl, combine the cornstarch and water until no clumps remain. Set aside.

4 Add the chickpeas to the skillet and stir. Next, add the coconut milk and the cornstarch solution. Mix thoroughly. Bring to a quick boil, then reduce heat to medium-low and simmer for 3 to 5 minutes.

5 Mix in the parsley and season to taste with salt, black pepper, and lemon or lime juice.

6 Serve with rice and a sprinkle of sesame seeds. Enjoy!

BAKED LEMON & DILL TEMPEH

PREP TIME: 20 MINUTES (PLUS 2
HOURS MARINATING TIME)
COOK TIME: 30 TO 45 MINUTES
YIELD: 4 SERVINGS

This dill and lemon marinated tempeh is inspired by Nordic and Scandinavian cuisine. It's also great for impressing your loved ones at the dinner table.

INGREDIENTS

2 (7- or 8-oz/200- or 250-g)
   tempeh* blocks

2 sheets roasted seaweed
   (nori or gim)

for the marinade:

zest and juice of 1½ lemons

¼ cup (3g) chopped dill, plus
   more for serving

¼ tsp salt

2 tsp ground sumac

¼ tsp chili flakes, more if
   desired

½ tsp paprika

1 tbsp maple syrup

4 tbsp olive oil

4 tbsp water

serving options:

1 to 2 tbsp vegan butter,
   melted

a few handfuls of fresh greens

4 to 6 tbsp vegan sour cream
   or hummus

4 to 6 medium potatoes,
   roasted, boiled or fried

1 Cut the two tempeh blocks lengthwise so each tempeh sheet is about ½ to 1 centimeter thick. Prick the four sheets with a fork. Then cut the sheets into any smaller shape you prefer (see photo 1). For a milder tempeh flavor, consider boiling the sheets for about 15 minutes.

2 Combine all the ingredients for the marinade in a small bowl.

3 Assemble the bake. Think of this as a lasagna. To an 8x8-in (20x20-cm) casserole or baking dish, add one sheet of seaweed. Then add half the tempeh pieces. Spoon half the marinade overtop. Add another sheet of seaweed. Then add the rest of the tempeh pieces and the rest of the marinade (see photo 2). Refrigerate for at least 2 hours, but no more than 24 hours.

4 Preheat your oven to 400°F (200°C). Bake for 25 to 30 minutes.

5 Serve topped with fresh dill and a drizzle of melted vegan butter on top, alongside fresh greens and vegan sour cream. This dish is also delicious with potatoes prepared however you like them. Enjoy!

Note:
   *Plain tofu works as a great substitute for the tempeh in this recipe.

TEMPEH PASTA SOUP

I'm a huge fan of this soup. The broth reminds me of chicken noodle soup, an all-time childhood favorite. Tofu makes a great tempeh substitute as well, if you prefer.

PREP TIME: 20 MINUTES
COOK TIME: 30 MINUTES
YIELD: 3 SERVINGS

INGREDIENTS

2½ tbsp olive oil

1 large yellow onion, roughly chopped

5.3oz (150g) celery root, chopped into 1-cm cubes

3 cloves garlic, peeled

1 tbsp nutritional yeast

2 tbsp white wine vinegar

1 tbsp maple syrup or brown sugar

5 cups (1,250ml) vegetable broth or vegan chicken stock, divided, plus more if needed

1 large carrot, diced small

1 leek, cut into rings

about 1 cup (200g) tempeh*, cut into 2-cm chunks

½ tsp marjoram, or dried herbs of choice

¼ tsp salt, or to taste

¼ tsp ground black pepper, or to taste

1 to 2 tsp hot sauce or a pinch of chili flakes (optional)

1 cup (100g) uncooked short cut pasta

1¼ cups (115g) broccoli, cut into bite-size florets

⅓ cup (10g) chopped parsley

1 Heat the olive oil in a medium or large pot on medium. Add the onion and celery root and cook for 5 to 7 minutes. Next, add the garlic and cook for another 2 to 3 minutes, stirring occasionally. Add the nutritional yeast, white wine vinegar, and syrup and cook 1 minute more. Then, pour in 1 cup (250ml) of the vegetable broth and stir.

2 Transfer the contents of the pot to a heatproof blender and blend on medium until smooth. Alternatively, use an immersion blender.

3 Pour the contents of the blender back into the pot and add 3 cups (750ml) of vegetable broth, plus the carrot, leek, and tempeh. Turn the heat up to high and bring to a boil. Cover with a lid, reduce heat to medium, and simmer 7 to 10 minutes, or until the carrot chunks are close to tender.

4 Season the broth with marjoram, salt, black pepper, and optional hot sauce. This may need a generous amount of salt, depending on the broth used.

5 Turn the heat up to high and add the remaining 1 cup (250ml) of broth. Bring the soup back up to a boil. Add the pasta, cover the pot, and let it cook until al dente.

6 Finally, reduce the heat to medium and add the broccoli florets. Cook 2 minutes, or until the broccoli is bright green and al dente. If your soup needs more liquid, adjust with another ½ cup to 1 cup of vegetable broth. Stir in the parsley and serve immediately!

Tip: If you're in Germany, simply use a packet of "Suppengemüse" for this recipe. This way, you have one leek, carrot, and celery root ready to go!

Notes:

*Tempeh comes with a slight bitterness. I personally don't mind it. I actually really like it and the taste reminds me of plain chicken. But if you are new to tempeh, or you know you are not the biggest fan, simply boil the tempeh chunks for 15 minutes in a small pot filled with water prior to adding them to your soup pot.

LENTIL PEANUT SOUP

PREP TIME: 15 MINUTES
COOK TIME: 30 MINUTES
YIELD: 3 TO 4 SERVINGS

INGREDIENTS

1 tbsp vegetable oil

1 onion, finely chopped

2 to 3 cloves garlic, finely chopped

1-inch piece ginger, peeled and finely chopped

1½ tbsp tomato paste/purée

1 tbsp soy sauce

½ tsp of ground cumin

½ tsp paprika

¼ tsp ground black pepper

¼ tsp ground turmeric

1 cup (190g) red, orange, or yellow lentils (the quick-cooking kind)

2 cups (500ml) vegetable broth

1 cup (250ml) water

2 tbsp peanut butter

2 tbsp fresh lemon juice

salt, to taste

1 to 2 tsp roasted sesame seeds per serving

handful of fresh parsley

4 to 6 slices of bread

Sometimes simple really is the best.

1   Heat the vegetable oil in a large saucepan on medium. Add the onion and sauté for 5 minutes. Stir in the garlic and ginger and let cook for an additional 2 minutes. Stir in the tomato paste and soy sauce. Cook 1 to 2 minutes more, then add the cumin, paprika, black pepper, and turmeric.

2   Add the lentils, broth, and water to the saucepan. Bring to a simmer. Cover with a vented lid and allow to simmer for about 20 minutes, stirring every 2 minutes. After 20 minutes, the lentils should have broken down completely. Remove from the heat.

3   Stir in the peanut butter and lemon juice. Then season with salt, to taste. If you prefer smoother soup, consider briefly blending. Serve immediately with sesame seeds, parsley, and bread.

LEMON TOFU

PREP TIME: 10 MINUTES
COOK TIME: 10 MINUTES
YIELD: 2 SERVINGS

INGREDIENTS

for the sauce:

1 tbsp cornstarch

⅓ cup (80ml) plus
  3 tbsp water, divided

½ tsp lemon zest

¼ cup (60ml) fresh lemon
  juice (1 to 2 lemons)

2 tbsp soy sauce

2 cloves garlic, minced

1 tsp sesame oil

¼ tsp chili flakes

2 tbsp sugar or agave

for the tofu:

3 tbsp cornstarch

1 tbsp nutritional yeast

¼ tsp ground black pepper

pinch of salt

7oz (200g) firm plain tofu,
  cut into chunks

1 to 2 tbsp vegetable oil, for
  frying

serving options:

1 green onion, finely
  chopped

sprinkle of sesame seeds

cooked quinoa, rice, or other
  grain of choice

vegetables of choice (raw,
  pickled, or stir-fried)*

This crispy tofu covered in a sticky and sour lemon sauce is one of my mom's favorite meals! She asks me to make it for her any time I'm home.

1 To make the sauce, in a small glass or bowl, combine the cornstarch and water until no clumps remain.

2 To a small saucepan, add the cornstarch mixture, ⅓ cup (80ml) water, lemon zest, lemon juice, soy sauce, garlic, sesame oil, chili flakes, and sugar. Mix well. Bring to a boil, stirring throughout. Reduce heat and simmer for 2 to 3 minutes, or until a thick consistency has been achieved.

3 For the tofu, in a medium bowl, combine the 3 tablespoons of cornstarch, yeast, black pepper, and salt. Add the tofu chunks and mix with a spoon, making sure to evenly coat each piece.

4 Heat the vegetable oil in a medium cast iron skillet on medium. Once hot, add the coated tofu chunks. Fry for 8 minutes, or until golden brown, moving them around often.

5 Either add the fried tofu chunks to the sauce directly or pour the sauce over the plated tofu. Sprinkle with green onion and sesame seeds. Serve with grain and vegetables of your choice. Enjoy!

Tip: Try serving this with the **Orange Bok Choy (page 121)** or the quick-pickled carrots on **page 96.**

POTATO & THYME GALETTE

PREP TIME: 35 MINUTES (PLUS
30 MINUTE FREEZE TIME)
COOK TIME: 70 MINUTES
YIELD: 4 TO 6 SERVINGS

INGREDIENTS

for the crust:

2¼ cups (270g) all-purpose flour

½ cup (60g) whole wheat flour

2 tbsp nutritional yeast

1 tsp salt

½ tsp garlic powder

1 tsp dried thyme

1 cup (225g) cold vegan butter (2 sticks)

3 to 5 tbsp nondairy milk

for the filling:

1 tbsp vegetable oil, plus more for the pan

2 large onions, diced

¼ cup (60ml) white wine

pinch of salt

pinch of ground black pepper

½ tsp dried thyme

5.3oz (150g) vegan cream cheese, vegan sour cream, or plain hummus

2 medium potatoes, thinly sliced

1 tbsp olive oil

Alright, this one is one of the fancier dishes this book has to offer. However, no special skills are required. The dough doesn't even need to be rolled out, just pressed into the pan. Easy peasy!

1 Start with the crust. To a food processor, add the flours, nutritional yeast, salt, garlic powder, and thyme, and blend.

2 Cut the cold vegan butter into small cubes and add those to the food processor. Pulse about 10 times until you have small chunks of butter evenly distributed in the flour mixture. Add 3 tablespoons of nondairy milk and pulse again a few times, adding more milk as needed until a smooth pie dough forms.

3 Transfer this mixture to a work surface and, with your hands, form it into a ball. Wrap the ball tightly in plastic wrap and place in the freezer for 30 minutes.

4 Meanwhile, to make the filling, heat the vegetable oil in a large skilley on medium. Once hot, add the onion and sauté for 8 to 10 minutes, or until lightly caramelized. Next, add the white wine, salt, black pepper, and thyme. Bring the heat to medium-high and simmer for 2 to 3 minutes, allowing most of the wine to evaporate. Remove from the heat and set aside.

5 Coat a 10-inch (26cm) springform pan with vegetable oil and preheat the oven to 350°F (180°C).

6 Add the cream cheese to the caramelized onions and mix together until well combined.

7 Remove the dough from the freezer. It should be firm but not frozen. Use about ⅔ of the dough to fill out the bottom of the springform pan. Simply pull chunks of dough from the ball and push them down into the bottom of the pan until the surface is covered. Use the remaining ⅓ of the dough to line the walls of the pan just over 1 inch (3cm) up on all sides (see photo 1).

8 Add the onion mixture to the crust and spread it evenly (see photo 2). Lay the potato slices on top of the filling (see photo 3). Carefully fold the dough walls inward so they're overlapping with the outer row of potatoes (see photo 4). Drizzle the olive oil over the potatoes. Sprinkle over an additional pinch of salt. Bake for 65 to 70 minutes.

9 Let the galette cool for about 15 minutes before cutting into it. Serve warm or cold with some fresh vegetables of choice.

ARTICHOKE TORTILLA PIZZA

PREP TIME: 15 MINUTES
COOK TIME: 15 MINUTES
YIELD: 1 TO 2 SERVINGS

These quick pizzas use crunchy fried tortillas as a base and come with a cheesy white artichoke and spinach topping.

INGREDIENTS

for the cheese sauce:

1 tbsp vegan butter

1 tbsp cornstarch

⅔ cup (160ml) nondairy milk

1 tbsp nutritional yeast

2 tsp white wine vinegar

pinch of salt, or to taste

¾ cup (75g) shredded vegan cheese

for the veggie mix:

1 tbsp olive oil

3 cloves garlic, finely minced

1 (14oz/400g) can artichoke hearts, drained and cut into small chunks

4 cups (100g) baby spinach

2 to 3 tbsp parsley, finely chopped

salt, to taste

ground black pepper, to taste

also:

3 tsp vegetable oil, for frying

3 10-inch (25cm) tortillas

serving option:

2 to 3 tbsp vegan Parmesan, (store-bought or recipe on **page 187**)

1 For the cheese sauce, heat the butter in a small saucepan on medium. Once the butter has melted, add the cornstarch and whisk thoroughly for one minute. Pour in the nondairy milk and continue mixing. Bring to a boil to activate the starch. Then, reduce the heat to medium and simmer for 2 to 3 minutes until it has thickened, mixing all throughout. Lastly, stir in the yeast, vinegar, salt, and shredded cheese. Set aside.

2 Heat the olive oil in a medium saucepan on medium. Once hot, add the garlic and cook for 2 minutes. Add the artichoke chunks and cook for 5 minutes, stirring occasionally and allowing some of the artichoke's moisture to evaporate. Next, add the spinach and parsley and continue to cook for 2 minutes. Season with salt and black pepper, to taste.

3 Add the cheese sauce to the artichoke mix and combine. Taste and adjust seasoning, if needed.

4 Heat 1 teaspoon vegetable oil in a nonstick skillet on medium. Add a tortilla and let it fry for 1 minute, or until the bottom is golden brown. Flip the tortilla and cook the opposite side equally. Repeat until all tortillas are fried.

5 Spread an equal portion of the cheese and artichoke mixture onto each toasted tortilla. Finish off with a sprinkle of vegan parmesan. Enjoy!

PRETZEL PIZZA

PREP TIME: 30 MINUTES (PLUS 2
  HOURS RISING TIME)
COOK TIME: 22 MINUTES
YIELD: 2 SERVINGS

INGREDIENTS

4 to 6 tbsp marinara sauce

for the dough:

¼ cup (60ml) nondairy milk

1 tbsp sugar

2 tbsp vegan butter

¼ cup (60ml) room
  temperature water

1½ tsp dry active yeast

1½ tsp salt

2 cups plus 1 tbsp (250g)
  white spelt flour or all-
  purpose flour

2 tsp olive oil, for kneading
  and oiling the bowl

for the cheese sauce:

2½ tsp vegan butter

2 tsp cornstarch

⅔ cup (160ml) unsweetened
  soy milk or soy cream

2 tsp white wine vinegar

2 tsp nutritional yeast

about ⅔ cup (60g) shredded
  vegan pizza cheese

pinch of salt, or to taste

for the baking soda solution:

1½ tbsp baking soda

½ cup (125 ml) water

optional toppings:

cherry tomatoes

sprinkle of dried Italian
  herbs

sun-dried tomatoes

vegan pepperoni

arugula or basil

Why not combine two of the greatest foods ever invented?

1 To prepare the dough, in a small saucepan, add the milk, sugar, and vegan butter. Heat on medium-high, letting the butter melt and the sugar dissolve for 1 to 2 minutes without letting it boil.

2 Pour the mixture into a large bowl and add the ¼ cup (60ml) of water. The temperature of the liquid should now be moderately warm. Sprinkle over the yeast and let sit for 5 to 10 minutes in a warm, protected spot, until frothy.

3 Combine the salt and flour in a medium bowl. Add this to the yeast mixture and stir until roughly combined. Next, transfer everything to your counter and knead with oiled hands for about 6 minutes until you have a smooth ball of dough.

4 Oil the bowl you just used and place the ball of dough inside. Cover and let rise for 1 to 2 hours in a warm space.

5 To prepare the cheese sauce, heat the vegan butter in a small saucepan on medium-high. Once the butter has melted, add the cornstarch and whisk thoroughly for about 1 minute until the starch is fully dissolved. Pour in the milk or cream and continue mixing. Add the vinegar, yeast, cheese, and salt. Bring to a boil to activate the starch, then reduce the heat to medium, allowing to simmer for about 2 minutes until thickened, stirring consistently. Set aside.

6 Preheat the oven to 425°F (220°C) and line 2 baking sheets with parchment paper.

7 Cut the dough in half. Transfer to a work surface and flatten each into a circular pizza crust. The thinner, the better! Transfer each crust to one of the prepared baking sheets.

8 To make the baking soda solution, add the baking soda and the ½ cup (125ml) water to a small saucepan and bring to a boil. Once the baking soda has fully dissolved, remove from the heat. Dip a baking brush into the solution and brush each crust completely with a thin coating of this solution.

9 Evenly spread about 2 to 3 tablespoons of marinara sauce to the center of the crusts. Add an equal amount of cheese sauce to each pizza, along with any toppings of choice. Bake for 10 to 15 minutes, or until deeply golden brown. Enjoy!

MY FAVORITE POTATO SALAD

PREP TIME: 10 MINUTES
COOK TIME: 25 MINUTES (PLUS
   25 MINUTES COOLING TIME AND
   2 HOURS IN THE FRIDGE)
YIELD: 3 TO 4 SERVINGS

INGREDIENTS

30oz (850g) small to medium
   yellow potatoes

½ cucumber, cut into small
   chunks (optional)

for the dressing:

½ cup (125g) think, plain soy
   yogurt

1½ tbsp vegan mayonnaise

1 tsp yellow mustard

¼ tsp smoked paprika

¼ tsp salt, or to taste

2 dashes ground black
   pepper, or to taste

1 tbsp white wine vinegar, or
   lemon juice, more to taste

1 tsp agave or maple syrup
   (optional)

1 small red onion, finely
   chopped

1 stalk of celery, finely
   chopped

1 tbsp fresh dill, finely
   chopped

2 tbsp chives, finely chopped

¼ cup (35g) dill pickles,
   finely chopped

A delicious German-style potato salad that makes me want to have a picnic in the sun—like right now!

1 Add the potatoes to a large pot of cold water and bring to a boil. Boil the potatoes for 15 to 20 minutes, or until tender.

2 To prepare the dressing, in a large salad bowl, combine the yogurt, mayonnaise, mustard, paprika, salt, black pepper, and vinegar. Consider adding some agave or maple syrup to balance out the tang. Add the onion, celery, dill, chives, and pickles to the dressing. Mix together and set aside.

3 Drain the potatoes and allow them to cool. If you prefer, peel the potatoes.

4 Chop the potatoes into bite-size chunks. Transfer the chunks to the bowl you made the dressing in. Mix well. Season with more salt, if necessary.

5 Let cool in the fridge for at least 2 hours. Just before serving, add the optional cucumber chunks to the salad as well. Enjoy!

Tip: Highly recommend serving this salad with some **Maple Mustard–Glazed Seitan Steaks (page 179)**!

1

2

MAPLE MUSTARD–GLAZED SEITAN STEAKS

PREP TIME: 25 MINUTES
COOK TIME: 30 MINUTES
YIELD: 4 TO 6 SERVINGS*

Making your own seitan may seem intimidating, but it's surprisingly easy! Plus, these steaks taste better than most supermarket alternatives out there. Trust me!

INGREDIENTS

1 to 2 tbsp vegetable oil, for grilling

for the seitan:

2 tbsp olive oil

4 tbsp white wine

4 tbsp soy sauce

2 tbsp yellow mustard

2 tbsp maple syrup

¼ tsp smoked paprika

½ tsp garlic powder

½ cup (125ml) vegetable broth

2 cups (260g) vital wheat gluten

for the glaze:

5 tbsp balsamic vinegar

2½ tbsp maple syrup

2 tbsp Dijon mustard

2 tbsp soy sauce

6 tbsp water

4 tsp cornstarch

serving options:

roasted potatoes

steamed broccoli

side salad

My Favorite Potato Salad (page 176)

1 To make the seitan, in a small saucepan, bring together the olive oil, white wine, soy sauce, yellow mustard, syrup, paprika, garlic powder, and vegetable broth. Bring to a simmer, whisking thoroughly, then remove from the heat.

2 Add the vital wheat gluten to a heatproof bowl. Pour in the contents of the saucepan. Mix thoroughly with a wooden spoon.

3 Once cool to the touch, transfer the mixture to a work surface and knead for about 8 minutes until it resembles photo 1.

4 Bring a small pot of salted water to a boil.

5 Cut the dough into 8 steak-like shapes (see photo 2) and add them to the pot to boil for about 20 minutes.

6 Meanwhile, in a small pot, combine all the ingredients for the glaze using a whisk. Bring to a quick boil on medium-high. Reduce heat to medium and keep whisking as you let simmer for 1 minute, or until it thickens. Remove from the heat.

7 Drain the steaks and pat them dry with a paper towel.

8 Heat the vegetable oil in a nonstick skillet on medium-high. Once hot, add the first batch of 4 steaks. Cook them for 2 to 3 minutes on each side, or until golden brown. Remove them from the pan and grill the second batch.

9 Pour half the glaze over the second batch of steaks and let cook for 2 to 3 minutes total, flipping the steaks half way through. Remove the glazed steaks from the pan. Add the remaining steaks and glaze to the pan and repeat. If your pan is big enough, cook all the steaks at once.

10 Consider serving with any of the optional sides. Enjoy!

Note:
*Cut the ingredients in half for a smaller serving size.

ONE POT HUMMUS RAMEN

PREP TIME: 15 MINUTES
COOK TIME: 30 MINUTES
YIELD: 2 TO 3 SERVINGS

This dish fuses the idea of ramen soup with warm Middle Eastern spices.

INGREDIENTS

2 tbsp olive oil, divided

2⅓ cups (200g) oyster mushrooms, cut into 1- to 2-cm strips

generous pinch of salt

¼ tsp ground black pepper

1 yellow onion, minced

¼ tsp red pepper flakes, or to taste

3 cloves garlic, minced

2 tsp tomato paste/purée

1 tbsp sugar

1 tbsp soy sauce

dash of sweet paprika

dash of ground cumin

dash of ground coriander

1 tsp tahini

2 tbsp plain hummus

1 tbso lemon juice

4 cups (1,000ml) vegetable broth, plus 1 to 2 additional cups (250ml to 500ml), if needed

2 blocks or 5.3 to 5.7oz (150 to 160g) dry ramen noodles

1 cup (35g) fresh baby spinach

2 green onions, chopped, plus more to serve

serving options:

roasted sesame seeds

chili flakes

1   Heat 1 tablespoon of olive oil in a large pot or skillet on medium-high. Add the mushrooms and cook them for 5 minutes until golden brown and crispy.* Next, stir in the salt and black pepper, remove the mushrooms from the pan, and set aside.

2   Reduce the heat to medium and heat the remaining tablespoon of olive oil. Add the minced onion and cook for about 5 minutes until translucent. Next, add the red pepper flakes and garlic and cook for another 2 minutes. Add the tomato paste, sugar, soy sauce, paprika, cumin, and coriander. Mix well and cook for another 1 to 2 minutes. Next, add the tahini, hummus, lemon juice, and 4 cups (1,000ml) vegetable broth. Turn the heat up to high and bring to a boil. Then reduce the heat to medium and simmer, covered, for 6 to 8 minutes. Season the broth to taste with salt.

3   Bring the broth up to a boil again, then add the noodles. Allow the noodles to boil, uncovered, for about 6 minutes, or until tender. About 1 minute before the noodles are done, add in the spinach, green onion, and cooked mushrooms. If needed, add more broth to adjust the soup to your liking. Season to taste once more and serve with sesame seeds, chili flakes, and extra green onion. Enjoy!

Tip: Spaghetti works as a substitute for the ramen noodles. Keep in mind it will need to cook in the broth a bit longer and therefore might need 1 to 2 extra cups of liquid.

Note:
   *The mushrooms will release quite a bit of moisture in the beginning before crisping up.

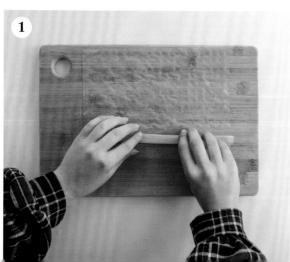

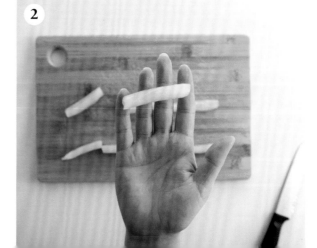

RICE PAPER TTEOKBOKKI SOUP

PREP TIME: 15 MINUTES
COOK TIME: 15 MINUTES
YIELD: 1 SERVING (2 SIDE
SERVINGS)

INGREDIENTS

1 small onion, diced

1 carrot, diced

2 cloves garlic, roughly chopped

2 tsp vegetable broth powder

½ tsp gochujang (Korean red chili paste), or to taste

1 tsp tomato paste

2 cups (500ml) water, plus more to adjust consistency, if needed

1 tsp rice vinegar

6 to 8 rice paper sheets (preferably square)

½ cup (80g) chickpeas, drained and rinsed

3.5oz (100g) firm or semi-firm tofu, cut into bite-size chunks

2 handfuls of fresh spinach

1 to 2 green onions, chopped

salt, to taste

roasted sesame seeds, for serving (optional)

I adore this soup. I make it for myself on a weekly basis. It's spicy, cozy, and incredibly satisfying.

1. In a small or medium saucepan, add the onion, carrot, garlic, vegetable broth powder, gochujang, tomato paste, water, and rice vinegar. Bring to a quick boil, stirring frequently. Then reduce heat to medium and simmer for about 10 minutes.

2. Meanwhile, to make the rice paper tteokbokki, fill a deep dish plate or shallow pan with room temperature water. Soak a rice paper sheet for 5 to 10 seconds, making sure it is fully submerged.

3. Transfer the sheet to a dry work surface. Roll it up tightly (see photo 1). It will soften as you work with it. Set aside and repeat until all sheets have been rolled. Once you have finished rolling, cut each roll into 2- to 3-inch-(5- to 7.5-cm)-long pieces (see photo 2).

4. Add the chickpeas, tofu chunks, and tteokbokki to the soup. Let simmer for about 2 minutes. If the soup needs more liquid at this point, add an extra splash of water. Lastly, add the spinach and green onion and allow everything to simmer for 2 more minutes. Season to taste with salt. Transfer to a bowl and sprinkle the sesame seeds over top, if desired. Enjoy!

BASIL "RICOTTA" PASTA

PREP TIME: 10 MINUTES
COOK TIME: 30 MINUTES
YIELD: 2 TO 3 SERVINGS

Tofu can be anything you want it to be, including delicious ricotta cheese!

INGREDIENTS

14oz (400g) firm plain tofu

3 tbsp cornstarch

1 heaping tbsp nutritional yeast

2½ tbsp olive oil

2 tbsp white wine vinegar

1 tsp salt

½ tsp garlic powder

¼ tsp ground turmeric

⅔ cup (160ml) nondairy milk

about ½ cup (10g) basil leaves

about ½ cup (15g) fresh baby spinach

7 to 8.8oz (200 to 250g) pasta

serving options:

additional fresh basil

½ cup (80g) cherry tomatoes, cut in half

pinch of red pepper flakes or paprika powder per plate

1 Preheat the oven to 350°F (180°C) and line an 8x8-inch (20×20-cm) baking dish with wet parchment paper (see pg.23).

2 To a food processor, add the tofu, cornstarch, yeast, olive oil, vinegar, salt, garlic powder, turmeric, milk, basil, and spinach. Blend until smooth. You'll have to scrape down the mixture a couple times. Pour the mixture into the prepared baking dish, smooth out the top, and bake for 30 minutes.

3 Meanwhile, cook the pasta according to package directions. Drain it, reserving about ½ cup (125ml) of the pasta water. Place the cooked pasta back into the empty pot.

4 Once the tofu has finished baking, scoop it from the baking dish and into the pasta pot. Mix well. If you'd like a thinner sauce, add the reserved pasta water a ¼ cup (60ml) at a time and mix until the sauce reaches your desired consistency. Taste and add more salt, if necessary.

5 Plate and serve with any of the optional toppings of choice. Enjoy!

MUSHROOM RAVIOLI

PREP TIME: 1 HOUR 15 MIN
COOK TIME: 25 MINUTES
YIELD: AROUND 20 RAVIOLI

INGREDIENTS

for the dough

1½ cup plus 1½ tbsp (200g) all-purpose flour

¾ cup (100g) wheat semolina flour

½ tsp salt

1¼ tbsp olive oil, plus more for kneading the dough

½ cup plus 1 tbsp (140ml) water

for the filling:

1 tbsp vegan butter

1 tsp olive oil

1½ cup plus 2 tsp (200g) mushrooms, finely chopped

2 cloves garlic, finely chopped

handful of chopped parsley

⅓ cup (80ml) soy cream

2 tsp nutritional yeast

zest of ½ lemon

salt, to taste

ground black pepper, to taste

2 tsp all-purpose flour

for the vegan Parmesan:

¾ cup (100g) cashews, roasted and salted

1 tbsp nutritional yeast

for the vegan garlic butter:

2 tbsp vegan butter

1 garlic clove, minced

Pro tip: Get a friend to join you in the making of this recipe! It's a bit more work intensive, but so, so worth it. My friend Artemis loves this one!

1 In a large bowl, combine the flour, semolina, and salt. Push the mixture toward the edges of the bowl, creating a well in the center. Add the oil and water to the center. Using a wooden spoon or spatula, slowly push the dry mixture toward the oil and water. Mix until a rough dough forms.

2 On a lightly floured work surface, knead the dough for 8 to 10 minutes with oiled hands. Once smooth, wrap it in parchment paper and cool in the fridge for 30 to 45 min.

3 To make the filling, heat the butter and olive oil in a medium skillet on medium. Add the mushrooms, letting them cook for about 5 minutes, stirring frequently. Add the garlic and parsley and let cook another 5 minutes. Mix in the soy cream and yeast. Add lemon zest, salt, and black pepper. Let cook for 2 minutes more before adding the final 2 teaspoons of flour.

4 To make the vegan Parmesan, add the roasted cashews and yeast to a food processor and blend until fine.

On a lightly floured work surface, roll out the cooled dough as thinly as possible. If you have a pasta machine, use that according to its instructions. The sheet of dough should be at least 12 x 16 inches (30 x 40cm). Using a cookie cutter or glass about 2½ inches (6cm) in diameter, punch out as many circles as you can in the flattened dough (see photo 1). Roll out the scraps and continue to punch out the rest of the circles as you go (see photo 2).

5 Time to assemble! Grab two pasta rounds and add 1 teaspoon of filling to the center of one. Place the second over top and close the edges using a fork (see photo 3). Repeat until all the ravioli have been assembled.

6 Bring a pot of salted water to a boil. Reduce to a simmer and add up to 10 ravioli to the pot at a time. Let each batch cook for about 3 to 5 minutes.

7 Meanwhile, to make the vegan garlic butter, add the butter and garlic to a small saucepan on medium and cook for 1 to 2 minutes. Drain each batch of ravioli and serve immediately, drizzled with melted garlic butter and sprinkled with vegan Parmesan. Enjoy!

OKONOMIYAKI

PREP TIME: 12 MINUTES
COOK TIME: 12 MINUTES
YIELD: 2 TO 3 LARGE PANCAKES

This roughly translates to "how you like it grilled" in Japanese. It's a delicious, savory pancake that comes with various toppings and fillings, as the name suggests.

INGREDIENTS

1 tbsp soy sauce

1 small handful of dried mushrooms (shiitake or morels)

1 sheet roasted seaweed (nori)

⅔ cup (160ml) hot water

1 cup plus 2 tbsp (150g) all-purpose flour

1½ tsp baking powder

½ tsp salt

1 tsp apple cider vinegar

3 tbsp unsweetened applesauce

1 cup (70g) shredded white cabbage

1 small carrot, grated

1 green onion, finely chopped, plus more for serving

2 tsp vegetable oil, for the pan

serving options:

crispy deep fried onions

vegan mayonnaise

a pinch of kala namak

vegan tonkatsu sauce

1 To make the broth, in a medium bowl, add the soy sauce, dried mushrooms, and seaweed. Add the hot water and let sit for 8 minutes.

2 Meanwhile, combine the flour, baking powder, and salt in a small bowl.

3 Remove the mushrooms and seaweed from the bowl and set aside. To the broth, add the vinegar and applesauce and mix well. Add in the flour mixture and stir until a thick batter forms. Once formed, let the batter rest for at least 5 minutes.

4 Meanwhile, chop the mushrooms and seaweed. Add these to the batter, along with the cabbage, carrot, and green onion.

5 Lightly brush a nonstick skillet with vegetable oil and heat on medium. Once hot, add ⅔ of the batter to the skillet. Using a rubber spatula, shape it into a pancake. Cook for 3 to 4 minutes, or until golden brown. Flip and cover with a lid, allowing the pancake to steam through for an additional 3 minutes.

6 Repeat step 5 for each pancake.

7 Serve immediately with any of the optional toppings. Enjoy!

Tip: Tonkatsu is a savory yet sweet condiment, oftentimes served with okonomiyaki. Simply combine 2 tablespoons of ketchup, 1 tablespoon of vegan worcestershire sauce, and 1 teaspoon of rice vinegar for a super-simple version of this sauce. Spread or drizzle it over the pancakes and then add your remaining toppings.

GREEN SPINACH RICE

PREP TIME: 15 MINUTES
COOK TIME: 30 MINUTES
YIELD: 2 TO 3 SERVINGS

This rice is among my top three favorite dishes in this book! There, I said it. It's so easy and simple. I highly recommend adding vegan feta for the perfect meal!

INGREDIENTS

1 cup (210g) rice, rinsed (preferably round short rice)

1¾ cup (430ml) water

pinch of salt, plus more to taste

2 tbsp olive oil

1 onion, finely chopped

2 cloves garlic, finely chopped

3.5oz (100g) fresh baby spinach, roughly chopped

¼ cup (60ml) white wine

pinch of red pepper flakes, or more to taste

2 tbsp hummus

1 tbsp lemon juice or white wine vinegar, more to taste

⅓ cup plus 2 tbsp (100ml) vegetable broth

handful of cherry tomatoes, halved

store-bought vegan feta cheese (optional)

1   In a medium pot, add the rice and water. Add a pinch of salt and stir once. Cover with a lid, and bring to a boil. Reduce the heat to medium-low and simmer for about 15 minutes, then take off the heat.* Allow the pot to sit, still covered, for 5 minutes until the rice is light and fluffy.

2   Heat the olive oil in a large skillet on medium. Once hot, add the onion, letting it sauté for 6 minutes. Next, add the garlic, allowing it to cook for another 2 minutes. Add the spinach and white wine. Let cook for another 2 to 3 minutes, or until the wine has mostly evaporated and the spinach has wilted. Finally, add the chili flakes, hummus, lemon juice, and vegetable broth. Mix well until the sauce becomes creamy.

3   Add the cooked rice to the sauce and mix again. Season to taste with salt and more lemon juice, if desired. Serve with some cherry tomatoes and the optional vegan feta cheese. Enjoy!

Note:
*Keep an eye on the pot. Toward the beginning of the cooking process, the water might start to overflow. Simply lift the lid for a few seconds when you feel like this is about to happen. Repeat as needed.

MAPLE & PECAN MILLET

PREP TIME: 10 MINUTES
COOK TIME: 30 MINUTES
YIELD: 2 SERVINGS

Craving breakfast for dinner? How about this bowl of spiced millet with buttery pecans and fresh berries?

INGREDIENTS

⅔ cup (130g) dry millet, rinsed

1 cup (250ml) water

1 tbsp vegan butter

⅓ cup (40g) raw pecans, roughly chopped

1 tbsp maple syrup

¼ tsp ground cinnamon

½ tsp vanilla extract

¼ tsp salt

¼ cup (40g) dates, pitted and chopped (deglet noor preferred)

½ cup (125ml) nondairy milk

serving options:

raspberries

puffed quinoa

splash of vegan cream

additional sprinkle of cinnamon

1 In a medium pot, add the millet and water and bring to a boil. Once boiling, cover with a lid* and reduce the heat to medium. Simmer for about 15 minutes, or until the water has been absorbed and the grain is close to being cooked through.** Turn off the heat. Making sure the pot is still covered, allow the millet to steam through for another 5 minutes.

2 Meanwhile, to a second medium pot, add the vegan butter and pecans. Heat on medium and let the pecans toast for about 2 minutes, stirring occasionally, until nice and fragrant.

3 Next, add the maple syrup, cinnamon, vanilla, salt, and chopped dates to the nuts. Mix well and allow to cook for another minute.

4 Add the milk and cooked millet. Cover and let cook for another 3 to 5 minutes on medium low.

5 Serve in two bowls with your preferred toppings. I suggest some fresh raspberries and vegan cream. Enjoy!

Note:

*I recommend using a lid with a small hole for the steam to escape.
**Keep an eye on the pot. Toward the beginning of the cooking process, the water might start to overflow. Simply lift the lid for a few seconds when you feel like this is about to happen. Repeat as needed.

ENCHILADA CRUNCH WRAPS

PREP TIME: 35 MINUTES
COOK TIME: 20 MINUTES
YIELD: 4 SERVINGS

INGREDIENTS

for the faux ground meat:

⅔ cup (45g) soy granules

¼ tsp vegetable broth powder

½ cup (125ml) boiling water

1 tbsp vegetable oil

for the enchilada sauce:

1 tbsp olive oil

¼ tsp chili flakes

½ tsp ground cumin

¼ tsp ground coriander

¼ white pepper

¼ ground black pepper

½ tsp paprika

½ tsp garlic powder

1 tsp sugar

⅓ cup (75g) tomato paste/
   purée

½ cup (125ml) vegetable
   broth

2 tsp cornstarch

¼ cup (60ml) water

¼ tsp salt, or to taste

for assembling the wraps:

5 to 6 large tortillas

20 tortilla chips or 4 small
   tostada shells

4 tbsp vegan cream cheese or
   vegan sour cream

2 medium tomatoes, sliced

4 handfuls of baby spinach

1 cup (100g) shredded vegan
   cheese

1 to 2 tbsp vegetable oil, for
   frying

These are so fun to make! Once you know how to fold these, they're easy to put together. If you need further assistance, a quick look at an online tutorial will help.

1 To make the faux ground meat, to a medium bowl or deep dish plate add the soy granules and vegetable broth powder. Give this a quick stir, then add the boiling water. Place a plate or lid on top to cover, and let this sit for about 5 minutes, or until the soy has cooked through.

2 Meanwhile, to make the enchilada sauce, in a saucepan or skillet on medium, add the olive oil, chili flakes, and spices. Cook for 1 minute and then mix in the sugar and tomato paste. Cook an additional 1 to 2 minutes, stirring frequently. Add the vegetable broth. In a small glass or bowl, combine the cornstarch and water until no clumps remain. Add this to the pot, stirring as you pour. Turn the heat to medium-high and simmer for 2 to 3 minutes, stirring often. Add salt, to taste.

3 To brown the ground soy, heat the vegetable oil in a nonstick skillet on medium-high. Drain the soy over a mesh strainer. Add the soy to the skillet and fry for about 3 minutes until golden brown. Once browned, add the granules to the enchilada sauce, mix it all up, and set aside.

4 In order for the crunch wraps to hold together, you'll need four circular tortilla cutouts 4 to 6 inches (10 to 15cm) in diameter. So grab 1 or 2 of the large tortillas and cut out those 4 circles. You can use a tostada as an outline while cutting. Alternatively, arrange 5 tortilla chips in a circle with the points touching, forming a pentagon, and cutting along the edges of the chips in a circular pattern.

5 Assemble! To the center of a tortilla, add one tablespoon of cream cheese, 2½ tablespoons of the enchilada sauce, 1 or 2 slices of tomato, a handful of spinach, 5 tortilla chips or a tostada shell, optional vegan cheese, and the tortilla cut out you made earlier (see photos 1 and 2). Following the circular shape, fold the edges of the tortilla inward, working clockwise (see photos 3 and 4). Repeat until you have 4 folded wraps.

6 Heat the vegetable oil in a nonstick skillet on medium-high. Fry each crunch wrap for a few minutes on each side until brown and crispy. Enjoy!

DESSERT

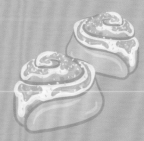

STRAWBERRY CHEESECAKE MOUSSE

PREP TIME: 7 MINUTES
COOK TIME: 30 MINUTES
    (PLUS 45 MINUTES COOL TIME)
YIELD: 4 TO 5 SERVINGS

INGREDIENTS

1 cup (150g) cashews

⅓ cup plus 1 tbsp (100g)
    thick, plain soy yogurt

5.3oz (150g) vegan cream
    cheese

1 cup (150g) frozen
    strawberries

pinch of salt

3 to 4 tbsp agave or maple
    syrup

1 tsp vanilla extract

for topping:

3 to 4 vegan graham crackers
    or cookies, crushed

½ cup (75g) chopped
    strawberries, fresh or
    frozen*

This light and creamy berry mousse is ridiculously easy—your blender is basically doing all the work here.

1   Boil the cashews in water for 30 minutes. Drain.

2   While the cashews are still hot, add them to a heatproof blender, followed by the yogurt, cream cheese, frozen berries, salt, syrup, and vanilla. Blend until smooth. If necessary, use a tamper to push down the ingredients as it is blending.

3   Scoop the mix into four small containers, such as ramekins or glasses. Smooth out the tops and refrigerate for at least 45 minutes.

4   Right before serving, top the desserts with crushed graham crackers and strawberry pieces. Enjoy!

Notes:

*If you are using frozen berries for the topping, let them thaw for about 15 minutes at room temperature before cutting into them.

PRETZEL BAKED CHEESECAKE

PREP TIME: 20 MINUTES
COOK TIME: 1 HOUR (PLUS 1 HOUR
    COOL TIME)
YIELD: 1 LARGE CHEESECAKE

A classic baked cheesecake, but with a tasty sweet and salty twist.

INGREDIENTS

vegetable oil or vegan butter,
    for the pan

for the pretzel crust:

7oz (200g) salty pretzels

½ cup (60g) all-purpose flour

⅓ cup (65g) sugar

½ cup plus 2½ tbsp (113g
    plus 2½ tbsp) softened
    vegan butter

4 to 6 tbsp nondairy milk

for the filling:

1 cup (250ml) soy cream

2½ cups plus ⅓ cup (700ml)
    thick, plain soy yogurt

1 tsp vanilla extract

⅔ cup plus ½ tbsp (160g)
    melted vegan butter

⅓ cup (80ml) agave syrup

¼ tsp salt

2 tbsp lemon juice

1½ tbsp sugar

⅔ cup (80g) cornstarch

serving options:

fresh berries

powdered sugar

1. Preheat the oven to 350°F (180°C) and line the bottom of a 10-inch (25-cm) springform pan with parchment paper. Additionally, oil the sides of the pan with a little vegetable oil.

2. In a food processor, blend the pretzels, flour, and sugar until fine. Add the butter and 4 tablespoons of nondairy milk and blend a few seconds more.

3. Remove the blade and test the consistency. The mixture should appear granular and stick together like coarse, wet sand. If not, add 2 more tablespoons of milk, one at a time.

4. Add the mixture to the springform pan and, with wet hands, press down firmly, dragging it up the sides about 1½ inch (3 to 4cm). Refrigerate for at least 10 minutes while you prepare the filling.

5. To make the filling, add the soy cream, soy yogurt, vanilla extract, butter, syrup, salt, lemon juice, and sugar to a blender and blend on low until combined. Add the cornstarch to the mixture and blend on medium until smooth.

6. Pour the filling into the crust. Bake for 1 hour.

7. Allow to cool completely on the counter. Once cooled, chill in the fridge for at least 1 hour. Carefully run a butter knife between the sides of the pan and the cheesecake before opening the springform pan. Feel free to serve with fresh berries and powdered sugar!

PEANUT BUTTER CHOCOLATE FUDGE BITES

PREP TIME: 10 MINUTES (PLUS
   15 MINUTES FREEZING TIME)
COOK TIME: NONE
YIELD: 2 TO 3 SERVINGS

INGREDIENTS

1 tbsp flax seed meal

2 tbsp unsweetened cocoa
   powder

pinch of salt

2 tbsp liquid sweetener

3 tbsp smooth peanut butter

½ tsp vanilla extract

1 to 2 tbsp additional cocoa
   powder or hemp seeds
   (optional)

The recipe for these little truffle bites is so simple! It only requires a handful of ingredients, all of which are likely to be hanging around your kitchen right now!

1   In a small or medium bowl, add all ingredients, except for the additional cocoa powder or hemp seeds. Mix well until smooth.

2   Place the bowl in the freezer for at least 15 minutes, but no more than 1 hour*.

3   Now shape 8 to 10 equal-size bites out of this mixture. Optionally, roll the bites in 1 to 2 tablespoons of cocoa powder or hemp seeds before serving. Store these in the fridge for up to a week or in the freezer for up to two weeks. Let thaw before serving.

Note:

*If you're short on time, feel free to not freeze this mixture and enjoy it immediately as a dip.

POPCORN PUDDING

PREP TIME: 12 MINUTES
COOK TIME: 12 MINUTES
YIELD: 2 SERVINGS

INGREDIENTS

1 tbsp coconut oil

¼ cup (32g) popcorn kernels

2 tbsp vegan butter

pinch of salt

1 tsp vanilla extract

2 to 3 tbsp sugar

1¾ cup (435ml) nondairy milk

¼ cup (30g) cornstarch

¼ cup (60ml) water

gold baking glitter (optional)

A custard for two made with a rich popcorn-infused milk, which has an amazing caramel flavor! As an added bonus, your kitchen is going to smell like heaven when you make this.

1 To make the popcorn, in a medium pot add the coconut oil and 2 popcorn kernels. Cover with a lid and heat on medium-high. Once the 2 kernels pop, turn the heat to medium-low and quickly add the remaining kernels. Cover again. Give the pan a quick shake to ensure the kernels are in one even layer. Continue shaking the pan as the kernels pop.

2 Once the kernels have stopped popping, take out 1 handful of popcorn and set that aside for serving later. To the pot with the remaining popcorn add the butter, salt, vanilla, sugar, and milk. Turn heat up to medium and simmer for 6 minutes.

3 Meanwhile, combine the cornstarch and water in a small bowl. Mix well until no more lumps remain.

4 Using a mesh strainer, strain the contents of the pot over a large bowl. Using the back of a spoon, press down on the popcorn, trying to squeeze out as much liquid as you can. Discard the strained popcorn.

5 Add the popcorn milk back into the pot you just used. Slowly pour in the cornstarch solution, stirring continuously.

6 Bring the heat to medium-high. Keep stirring, as the mixture simmers for about 2 minutes or until it reaches a pudding-like consistency.

7 Transfer the mixture to two 6oz (180ml) ramekins or glasses. To serve cold, refrigerate for at least 30 minutes before serving. Decorate with the popcorn you set aside earlier and some optional gold baking glitter. Enjoy!

CHOCOLATE CHIP OAT COOKIES

PREP TIME: 8 MINUTES (PLUS 15
    MINUTES FREEZING TIME)
COOK TIME: 10 MINUTES
YIELD: 10 TO 12 COOKIES

INGREDIENTS

2⅔ cups (240g) old-fashioned
    or quick-cooking oats

½ tsp salt

1 tsp baking powder

1 tsp vanilla extract

¼ tsp ground cinnamon

½ cup (95g) coconut sugar or
    brown sugar*

¼ cup plus 1 tbsp (70g) vegan
    butter, softened

3 tbsp unsweetened
    applesauce

¼ cup (60ml) nondairy milk

⅓ cup (60g) chocolate chips

This is an incredibly reliable cookie recipe that everyone should have in their recipe box. Enough said!

1 To a food processor, add all ingredients except the chocolate chips. Blend until as smooth as possible. Stir in the chocolate chips by hand.

2 Chill the batter in the freezer for 15 to 20 minutes. The mixture can also be prepared in advance and kept in the fridge for a minimum of 1 hour and a maximum of 24 hours.

3 Preheat the oven to 375°F (190°C) and line a baking sheet with parchment paper.

4 Measure out the cookies using an ice cream scoop or tablespoon. Each cookie should be about one scoop of dough or 1½ tablespoons. Place the scoops on the sheet. Leave about 2 inches of room between each scoop. Using your hands, flatten each scoop into a ½ inch thick disk.

5 Bake for around 15 minutes or until the edges start to darken and turn golden brown.

6 Let cookies rest for at least 10 minutes before serving. They will set and crisp up a bit more when cooling. Enjoy with a cold cup of oat milk!

Tip: If you're not in the mood to bake, the cookie batter can be served on its own after freezing for at least 20 minutes.

Note:

*Coconut sugar will give these a more subtle sweetness. Brown sugar will make these a bit sweeter while allowing for a nice chewy texture.

SWEET & SALTY ALMOND COOKIES

PREP TIME: 15 MINUTES
COOK TIME: 12 TO 15 MINUTES
YIELD: 4 TO 5 COOKIES

INGREDIENTS

1½ tbsp ground flax seeds

2 tbsp water

¼ cup (50g) brown sugar

2 tbsp softened vegan butter

1 tsp vanilla extract

⅓ cup (80g) almond butter

3 drops almond extract

½ cup (60g) all-purpose flour
   or white spelt flour

¼ cup (35g) ground almonds

½ tsp baking powder

½ tsp salt

optional add-ins:

chocolate chips

chopped almonds

dried cherries

raisins

apple chunks

This recipe yields a small batch of sweet and salty cookies. The added almond extract provides a subtle marzipan flavor—perfect for cozy winter nights.

1 Add the flax seeds and water to a medium or large bowl. Let sit for 5 minutes.

2 Meanwhile, preheat the oven to 375°F (190°C) and line a baking sheet with parchment paper.

3 To the flax seeds, add the brown sugar, vegan butter, vanilla, almond butter, and almond extract. Mix well using a whisk or electric hand mixer.

4 Add the flour, ground almonds, baking powder, and salt. Mix again until roughly combined. Next, add a small handful of any of your desired add-ins. Using your hands, gently mix everything together until a thick dough forms.

5 Still using your hands, shape the dough into 4 or 5 large, thick mounds, placing each onto the baking sheet with equal distance between them.

6 Bake for 12 to 15 minutes. Let sit for at least 30 minutes before serving. Enjoy!

SWEET POTATO MARBLED MUFFINS

PREP TIME: 15 MINUTES
COOK TIME: 35 MINUTES
YIELD: 10 MUFFINS

INGREDIENTS

for the sweet potato batter:

1 (4 to 5 oz/113 to 140g)
  sweet potato, peeled

2 tsp vanilla extract

1 tsp apple cider vinegar

⅔ cup (160ml) nondairy
  milk

⅓ cup plus 2 tsp (90ml)
  vegetable oil, plus more for
  pan, if needed

2 cups plus 1 tbsp (250g)
  white spelt flour or all-
  purpose flour

¾ cup (150g) sugar

½ tsp salt

2 tsp baking powder

1 tsp ground cinnamon

½ tsp pumpkin pie spice

for the chocolate swirl:

2½ tbsp unsweetened cocoa
  powder

3 tbsp nondairy milk

1 tbsp maple syrup

a handful of chopped
  walnuts

¼ cup (45g) vegan chocolate
  chunks

Walnuts, sweet potato, chocolate, and cinnamon. These muffins are as autumnal as it gets!

1 Cut the sweet potato into bite-size chunks. In a small pot, boil the sweet potato chunks for 12 to 15 minutes, or until tender.

2 Meanwhile, preheat the oven to 350°F (180°C) and oil 10 muffin cups, or line them with muffin liners.

3 Drain the sweet potatoes and transfer them to a large plate. Using a fork, mash until smooth. Measure out ⅓ cup plus 1 tablespoon (90g) of the mashed potato and transfer to a medium bowl. The rest can be stored in the fridge in an airtight container for up to 3 days. Add the vanilla, vinegar, milk, and vegetable oil to the sweet potato and stir.

4 In a large bowl, combine the flour, sugar, salt, baking powder, cinnamon, and pumpkin pie spice. Add in the sweet potato mixture and mix until smooth.

5 Add a heaping tablespoon of batter to each of the prepared muffin cups, making sure there is some batter left over.

6 In a small bowl, whisk together the cocoa powder, milk, and syrup until smooth. Add this chocolate mixture to the remaining batter in the bowl and mix. Once mixed, add it evenly to the muffin cups. Using a butter knife, lightly swirl the two parts together. Less is more here, as you still want to see the layering of colors in the muffins.

7 Lastly, add the walnuts and chocolate chunks to each of the muffins, sprinkling over the tops. Bake for 20 to 25 minutes. Let cool for 30 minutes before removing the muffins from the pan. Enjoy!

DATE & MAPLE CRUMBLE BARS

PREP TIME: 12 MINUTES
COOK TIME: 40 MINUTES
YIELD: 9 BARS

INGREDIENTS

for the dough:

2 tbsp ground flax seeds

½ cup (125ml) maple syrup

½ cup (125ml) nondairy milk

2 tsp vanilla extract

½ cup (135g) melted vegan butter

2¼ cups (270g) all-purpose flour

1½ cups (135g) quick-cooking oats

1 tsp baking powder

1 tsp salt

for the date filling:

8.5oz (250g) dates, pitted (deglet noor preferred)

⅓ cup (80ml) maple syrup

pinch of salt

¼ cup (60ml) nondairy milk

One of my favorite treats from this book, this recipe has two layers of vanilla crumble dough with a delicious date mixture stuffed between. Sweet, but not too sweet. I'm in love, what can I say?

1 Add the dates to a medium bowl, cover with boiling water, and allow to soak for 15 minutes. Then drain and set aside.

2 In a large bowl, combine the flax seeds, maple syrup, nondairy milk, and vanilla. Add in the melted butter and stir well.

3 Now add the flour, oats, baking powder, and salt. Mix well. Refrigerate the dough while you prepare the date filling.

4 Add the dates, maple syrup, salt, and milk to a food processor. Blend until you've got a smooth, yet sticky, paste. A few chunks in the paste are completely fine.

5 Preheat the oven to 350°F (180°C) and line an 8x8-inch (20x20-cm) baking pan with wet parchment paper (see p.23). Make sure you leave parchment paper hanging over the sides of the pan to make it easier to lift out later.

6 Press a little over half the oat batter evenly into the baking pan. Add the date filling on top and use a spatula to smooth it into an even layer. Using your hands, crumble the remaining batter over top.

7 Bake for 35 to 38 minutes, or until golden brown. Let cool for at least 30 minutes. Lift out of the baking dish, cut into nine equal squares, and serve.

PUMPKIN SWIRL BROWNIES

PREP TIME: 12 MINUTES
COOK TIME: 35 MINUTES
YIELD: 9 BROWNIES

INGREDIENTS

for the brownie mix:

1 cup plus 1 tbsp (125g plus 1 tbsp) all-purpose flour

½ cup minus 2 tsp (45g) unsweetened cocoa powder

1 tsp baking powder

½ tsp salt

½ tsp ground cinnamon or pumpkin pie spice

1 cup minus 1 tbsp (185g) sugar

½ tsp vanilla extract

2.5oz (70g) pumpkin puree

½ cup (125ml) sunflower seed oil

½ cup (125ml) nondairy milk

for the pumpkin swirl:

5.5oz (150g) pumpkin puree

3 tbsp thick, plain soy yogurt

3 tbsp melted vegan butter

2 tbsp sugar

½ tsp ground cinnamon or pumpkin pie spice

This recipe is my pride and joy! It's had a slight update since debuting on my YouTube channel. This truly is the best brownie recipe there is, provided you enjoy a rich, fudgy brownie with pumpkin pie swirls running through it.

1 Preheat the oven to 350°F (180°C) and line an 8x8-inch (20x20-cm) baking pan with wet parchment paper (see p.23). Make sure you leave parchment paper hanging over the sides of the pan to make it easier to lift out later.

2 In a large bowl, combine the flour, cocoa powder, baking powder, salt, cinnamon, and sugar.

3 Next, add the vanilla, pumpkin puree, sunflower seed oil, and milk. Thoroughly mix with an electric hand mixer.

4 Pour the batter into the baking dish, reserving 5 tablespoons of batter in the mixing bowl. Smooth out the top of the batter in the baking dish and set aside.

5 In a small bowl, combine the ingredients for the pumpkin swirl mix.

6 Spoon the pumpkin mixture over the top of the unbaked brownie batter in small dollops (see photo 1). Next, spoon the brownie batter that was set aside into the spaces between the pumpkin dollops (see photo 2).

7 Carefully drag a butter knife in a wavelike motion over the top to create a swirl pattern (see photo 3). Be sure not to swirl the mixtures together too much, as you still want to distinguish the separate layers.

8 Bake for 30 to 35 minutes. Let cool on the counter for at least 20 minutes, then transfer to the fridge to cool for an additional 2 hours. Enjoy!

Tip: I like to crush vegan black and white sandwich cookies and sprinkle them along the edges of the brownies before baking to add an extra layer of sweetness!

1

2

3

APPLE PIE MILKSHAKE

PREP TIME: 10 MINUTES
COOK TIME: NONE (6 HOURS
  FREEZING TIME PLUS 30 MINUTES
  BOILING TIME)
YIELD: 2 SERVINGS

INGREDIENTS

1½ apples

¼ cup (40g) cashews, soaked
  in water overnight or
  boiled for 20 to 30 minutes

3 soft dates or 1 tbsp maple
  or agave syrup

¼ tsp ground cinnamon, plus
  a pinch more, for serving

pinch of salt

½ tsp vanilla extract

2½ tbsp vegan sour cream,
  cream cheese, or thick,
  plain soy yogurt

⅔ cup (160ml) nondairy
  milk

This shake tastes like a slice of apple pie topped with vanilla ice cream. Frozen apple slices are the secret ingredient.

1 Ahead of time, cut the apples into thin slices and freeze them for at least 6 hours. To prevent apple slices from sticking together when freezing, place them on a baking sheet with parchment paper, leaving space between slices.

2 Also ahead of time, soak the cashews in water for at least 6 hours. Alternatively, boil them for 20 to 30 minutes, right before blending in step 4. I recommend boiling the cashews to ensure a smoother blend.

3 If using dates, soak them in boiling water for 15 minutes. Drain.

4 Add the frozen apples, drained cashews, and all other ingredients to a blender and blend until smooth. Serve immediately with a sprinkle of cinnamon on top. Enjoy!

BITTERSWEET HAZELNUT MOUSSE

PREP TIME: 5 MINUTES
COOK TIME: 5 MINUTES
YIELD: 4 TO 6 SERVINGS

INGREDIENTS

⅔ cup (125g) dark chocolate, broken into bits

14oz (400g) silken tofu

¾ cup (225g) vegan chocolate hazelnut spread

pinch of salt

serving options:

roasted hazelnuts, peeled and crushed

berries, fresh, dried, or frozen

cocoa nibs

vegan whipped cream

This luxurious, bittersweet chocolate mousse uses only a short list of ingredients. I made this for my neighbor once and he's still raving about it to this day.

1 Melt the chocolate.*

2 To a blender or food processor, add the tofu, melted dark chocolate, hazelnut spread, and salt. Blend on high until smooth.

3 Divide this mix evenly between 4 to 6 small glasses or ramekins. Place those in the fridge to set for at least 45 minutes before serving.

4 Feel free to top with plant-based whipped cream, berries, cocoa nibs, roasted hazelnuts, or anything else you desire! Enjoy!

Notes:

*__Microwave Method:__ Place the chocolate in a microwave-safe bowl. Microwave for 30 seconds at a time, removing and stirring between, until the chocolate has melted thoroughly.

*__Oven Method:__ Melt the chocolate in the oven in a medium oven-proof bowl at 300°F (150°C) for 5 minutes. Carefully remove the bowl and let sit for 5 minutes before mixing the chocolate until fully melted.

MOCHA CUPCAKES

PREP TIME: 12 MINUTES
COOK TIME: 15 MINUTES
YIELD: 12 CUPCAKES

Allow me to introduce you to some fudgy mocha cupcakes. Subtly sweet and paired with a dark and rich chocolate flavor, these are sure to delight.

INGREDIENTS

1½ cups (150g) dark chocolate, broken into bits

2 cups (240g) flour

½ cup plus 2 tbsp (130g) sugar

2 tbsp unsweetened cocoa powder, plus more for serving

1 tbsp finely ground espresso or coffee powder

1 tsp baking powder

½ tsp salt

⅓ cup plus 1½ tbsp (100ml) vegetable oil, plus more for pan

1¼ cups (310ml) brewed coffee

¾ cup plus 2 tbsp (200ml) vegan whipped cream or instant soy whip

1 to 2 tsp agave syrup

1 Preheat the oven to 350°F (180°C) and grease 12 muffin cups with vegetable oil or line them with muffin liners.

2 Melt the chocolate.*

3 In a large bowl, combine the flour, sugar, cocoa powder, espresso powder, baking powder, and salt. Add the melted chocolate, oil, and coffee and, using an electric mixer, mix until smooth.**

4 Divide the batter evenly between the muffin cups. Bake for 15 minutes. Let cool for at least 30 minutes.

5 Meanwhile, in a large bowl, whip up the cream. Add 1 to 2 teaspoons of agave syrup, or to taste.

6 To remove the cake, carefully run a knife along its edges and lift it out. Add about 1 to 2 heaping tablespoons of the cream on top of each cake and dust with cocoa powder. Enjoy!

Notes:

*Microwave Method: Place the chocolate in a microwave-safe bowl. Microwave for 30 seconds at a time, removing and stirring between, until the chocolate has melted thoroughly.

*Oven Method: Melt the chocolate in the oven in a medium oven-proof bowl at 300°F (150°C) for 5 minutes. Carefully remove the bowl and let sit for 5 minutes before mixing the chocolate until fully melted.

** Alternatively, add all the ingredients for the batter to a large blender and blend for a few seconds until smooth!

LEMON & GINGER LOAF

PREP TIME: 12 MINUTES
COOK TIME: 55 MINUTES
YIELD: 10 TO 12 SLICES

This is a bright and fluffy lemon loaf covered in a gingery donut glaze. Adding edible flowers as decoration is optional, but highly recommended.

INGREDIENTS

for the loaf:

½ cup plus 2½ tbsp (135g) sugar

⅓ cup (80ml) vegetable oil or melted vegan butter

2 tbsp applesauce

zest of 1 lemon

2 tbsp lemon juice

2 tsp grated ginger

⅔ cup (160ml) nondairy milk

2 cups (240g) all-purpose flour

2 tsp baking powder

½ tsp salt

for the glaze:

2 tbsp vegan butter

1 inch (2.5cm) piece of ginger, peeled

½ tsp fresh lemon zest

¾ cup (90g) powdered sugar

1 to 2 tbsp nondairy milk

serving options:

1 to 2 tbsp edible flowers**

½ tsp lemon zest

1 In a large bowl, combine the sugar, oil, applesauce, lemon zest, lemon juice, ginger, and milk. Allow to curdle for 5 to 10 minutes.

2 Meanwhile, preheat the oven to 350°F (180°C) and line an 8-inch (20-cm) loaf pan with wet parchment paper (see p.23). Make sure you leave parchment paper hanging over the sides of the pan to make it easier to lift out later.

3 In a small bowl, combine the flour, baking powder, and salt.

4 Combine the dry and wet ingredients and mix everything until smooth. Be sure not to overmix. Pour the batter into the loaf pan and smooth out the top.

5 Bake for 50 to 55 minutes, or until a toothpick inserted into the center comes out clean. Let cool on the counter for at least 30 minutes.

6 Prepare the glaze while the loaf is cooling down. To a small saucepan on medium, add the vegan butter, ginger, and lemon zest. Cook for 3 minutes to infuse the butter with lemon and ginger flavor. Then carefully remove and discard the piece of ginger.* Remove the pot from the heat and add the powdered sugar. Whisk thoroughly. Add the milk 1 tablespoon at a time until a thin glaze forms.

7 Once you have carefully lifted the cake out of the pan, and it has cooled down completely, pour over the glaze. Allow the glaze and cake to set in the fridge for at least 30 min. This tastes best after it has been cooling in the fridge for a couple hours.

Tip: Feel free to go one step further and decorate the cake with edible flowers and additional lemon zest! Add this additional decoration right after pouring the glaze on top.

Notes:

*You can also rinse the piece of ginger and use it to make ginger tea!

**Add the edible flowers before the glaze has set.

HALF-BAKED CHERRY CHOCOLATE CHEESECAKE

This cake is a dream! Anyone want to bake this for my birthday?

PREP TIME: 20 MINUTES (PLUS 10 HOURS COOLING TIME)
COOK TIME: 30 MINUTES (PLUS 30 MINUTES BOILING TIME)
YIELD: 1 MEDIUM CHEESECAKE

INGREDIENTS

for the cake base:

⅓ cup plus 1 tbsp (90g) vegan butter, plus more for the pan

⅓ cup (80ml) nondairy milk

1 tsp vanilla extract

½ cup (100g) sugar

1 tbsp ground flax seeds

¼ cup (25g) unsweetened cocoa powder

¾ cup (90g) all-purpose flour

1 tsp baking powder

¼ tsp salt

½ cup (85g) chocolate chips

for the cheesecake filling:

1¼ (175g) cup cashews

10.5oz (300g) vegan cream cheese

½ cup plus ½ tbsp (70g) powdered sugar

pinch of salt

1 tsp vanilla extract

1 tbsp lemon juice

3 tbsp softened vegan butter

for the topping:

1½ cup (225g) frozen cherries, pitted

2 tbsp sugar

1 tsp vanilla extract

2 tsp cornstarch

¼ cup (60ml) water

1 Line the bottom of an 8-inch (20-cm) springform pan with parchment paper. Coat the sides of the pan well with vegan butter. Preheat the oven to 350°F (180°C).

2 Melt the vegan butter in a small saucepan. Meanwhile, in a large bowl, combine the milk, vanilla, and sugar. Pour in the melted butter. Mix in the flax seeds and set aside.

3 In a smaller bowl, combine the unsweetened cocoa, all-purpose flour, baking powder, and salt. Add to the wet ingredients and combine until smooth. Be careful not to overmix. Fold in the chocolate chips. Pour into the springform pan, smooth the top, and bake for 25 minutes.

4 Meanwhile, boil the cashews in a medium saucepan for 25 to 30 minutes. Then drain.

5 Remove the cake base from the oven and let cool completely.

6 In a large blender, add the ingredients for the filling and blend until smooth. Next, pour the filling over top of the cake base and refrigerate for at least 10 hours.

7 The next day, prepare the topping. Add the frozen cherries, sugar, and vanilla to a small saucepan on medium-high, letting the fruit defrost and cook for 2 minutes.

8 Meanwhile, in a small glass or bowl, combine the cornstarch and water until no clumps remain. Add this cornstarch mixture to the saucepan with the fruit. Bring to a quick boil, then reduce the heat to medium, simmering for another 2 minutes. Remove from the heat. For a smooth topping, blend in a heat-proof blender for a few moments.

9 Carefully run a butter knife along the cake's edges, separating it from the springform pan. Then open the pan and lift the top off the sides.*

10 Pour the cherry topping over the cheesecake and serve. Leftovers can be stored in the fridge for up to 2 days.

Note:

*I highly recommend placing the cake in the freezer for 30 minutes to 1 hour prior to opening the springform pan and adding the topping. This will ensure the pan releases the cake more easily.

MANGO RICE PAPER TREATS

PREP TIME: 15 MINUTES
COOK TIME: 12 MINUTES
YIELD: 1 TO 2 SERVINGS

These crispy mango treats covered in sweet coconut sauce are my go-to single serving dessert. I make these all the time for myself, sometimes adding banana or pineapple. Treat yourself!

INGREDIENTS

6 to 8 small round rice paper wrappers, about 6 inch (15cm) in diameter

1 cup (135g) frozen mango

1 to 3 tsp coconut oil

sprinkle of sesame seeds, for serving

for the sauce:

2 tbsp water

1 tsp cornstarch

⅓ cup (80ml) coconut milk

1 to 2 tsp maple or agave syrup

½ tsp vanilla extract

pinch of salt

1   Fill a deep dish plate with room temperature water. Add 1 rice paper sheet to the water. Let it soak for 5 to 10 seconds, fully submerged.

2   Transfer the rice paper to a smooth surface, such as a cutting board. It will soften up as it sits. Add about 3 frozen mango pieces to the center of the rice paper and wait for it to soften up just enough for you to be able to fold it.

3   Roll the wraps like you would a burrito. Fold over the lower end of the rice paper, pulling the filling toward yourself (see photo 1). Next, fold over the sides (see photo 2). Finally, roll it up in the opposite direction, away from yourself (see photo 3).

4   Repeat steps 1 through 3 until all treats have been prepared. Be sure the uncooked rolls don't touch, as they will stick together easily.

5   Heat 1 to 2 teaspoons of coconut oil in a nonstick skilled on medium-high. It is best to cook in two batches. Cook each batch for 5 minutes, moving the treats around to ensure all sides are cooked evenly. If needed, add another teaspoon of coconut oil to the second batch. They should all come out golden brown and crispy.

6   To prepare the sauce, in a small glass or bowl, combine the cornstarch and water until no clumps remain. In a small pot on high, stir together the milk, syrup, vanilla, salt, and cornstarch mixture. Bring to a boil, stirring throughout. Reduce heat to medium and simmer for about 1 minute, then remove from the heat.

7   Serve your rice paper bites with the sauce poured over top or on the side for dipping. Sprinkle sesame seeds over top.

CARROT CAKE FOR ONE

PREP TIME: 5 MINUTES
COOK TIME: 2 MINUTES
 (MICROWAVE) OR 35 MINUTES
 (CONVENTIONAL OVEN)
YIELD: 1 SERVING

INGREDIENTS

1 tbsp vegetable oil, plus
  1 tsp more for the pan

2½ tbsp shredded carrot

½ tsp vanilla extract

1 tbsp plus 1 tsp (16g) sugar

¼ cup (60ml) nondairy milk

¼ cup (35g) all-purpose flour

2 tbsp plus 1 tsp quick-
  cooking oats

¼ tsp baking powder

pinch of salt

pinch of ground nutmeg

½ tsp ground cinnamon

1 tbsp raisins (optional)

1 tbsp chopped nuts
  (optional)

serving options:

2 tbsp plain or vanilla vegan
  yogurt or softened vegan
  cream cheese

drizzle of maple syrup

1 tbsp chopped walnuts

Sometimes all you need is an entire carrot cake only for you—and you alone.

1 Using 1 teaspoon of vegetable oil, coat a small oven-proof ramekin, mug, or bowl that has at least ½ cup (125ml) capacity.

2 If you're using the oven*, preheat to 350°F (180°C).

3 In a small bowl, add the shredded carrot, vanilla, 1 tablespoon of oil, sugar, and milk, and mix together.

4 Next, add the flour, oats, baking powder, salt, and spices. Feel free to add raisins and chopped nuts if you choose. Mix together and pour the contents into the baking container.

5 The cooking time can vary depending on your baking container. If using the oven, bake for 30 to 40 minutes. If using the microwave, cook for about 2 minutes. Check the consistency as needed when using either method.

6 Let the cake cool for at least 10 minutes. To remove the cake, carefully run a knife along its edges and lift it out.

7 Top with some plain or vanilla vegan yogurt, maple syrup, and chopped nuts, if desired.

Note:
*I prefer the baked version a little more, it comes out extra fluffy!

APRICOT, TAHINI & OAT BUNS

PREP TIME: 25 MINUTES (PLUS
    2 HOURS 15 MIN RISING TIME)
COOK TIME: 25 MINUTES
YIELD: 7 ROLLS

INGREDIENTS

½ cup (125ml) nondairy
    milk

¼ cup (60ml) agave or maple
    syrup

1 tsp vanilla extract

1½ tbsp white tahini

2 tbsp vegan butter, plus
    more for the pan and
    brushing

1½ tsp (3.5g) active dry yeast

2 cups (240g) all-purpose
    flour

½ cup (45g) quick-cooking
    oats

½ tsp ground cinnamon

½ tsp salt

1 to 2 tsp oil, for kneading

sesame seeds, for serving

for the filling:

2 tsp white tahini

2½ tbsp apricot jam, plus
    more for serving

2 to 3 apricots, cut into
    chunks (optional)

for the glaze:

1½ tbsp white tahini

1½ tbsp agave or maple syrup

pinch of salt

1 to 2 tsp nondairy milk

These rolls are incredibly fluffy and not too sweet. The oats and tahini add a subtle heartiness to the dough, which makes these perfect for breakfast as well, provided you made them ahead of time.

1   In a small saucepan, combine the milk, syrup, vanilla, tahini, and vegan butter. Heat on medium-high for 1 to 2 minutes, or until the butter has melted. Transfer the mixture to a large bowl and let cool until it is lukewarm to the touch, or 105 to 110°F (40 to 43°C). Sprinkle the yeast over top. Let sit for 5 to 10 minutes, in a warm, protected spot until frothy.

2   In a medium bowl, mix together the flour, oats, cinnamon, and salt. Add the dry ingredients to the yeast and mix with a wooden spatula or spoon until the dough begins to form.

3   Transfer the dough to a work surface and lightly coat your hands in oil. Knead it for 5 minutes. Then, place the dough in an oiled bowl and let it rise somewhere warm for 60 minutes.

4   Meanwhile, coat an 8- or 9-inch (20- or 22.5-cm) baking dish with vegan butter.

5   On a lightly floured cutting board, roll the dough into a rectangle about 11x8 inches (28x20cm) in size. Spread tahini and apricot jam evenly over the dough (see photo 1). Cut the dough vertically into 7 strips of equal size (see photo 2) and tightly roll up each one (see photo 3). By rolling each piece individually, you prevent the filling from oozing out too much.

6   Transfer the rolls to the prepared baking dish. If you would like, tuck a few apricot pieces inside each roll. Place the rolls in a warm, protected spot to rise for 60 to 75 minutes until they've almost doubled in size.

7   Preheat the oven to 350°F (180°C) and brush the buns with about 1 tablespoon of melted vegan butter.

8   Bake for 20 to 25 minutes, or until golden brown.

9   In a small bowl, combine the ingredients for the glaze. Drizzle over top. Cut the buns and carefully lift them out of the pan.

10 Serve fresh with some more apricot jam and a sprinkle of sesame seeds for a nice presentation.

CHOCOLATE CHAI ICE CREAM

PREP TIME: 5 MINUTES
COOK TIME: 5 MINUTES (PLUS 4
   HOURS FREEZING TIME)
YIELD: 4 SERVINGS

INGREDIENTS

½ cup (75g) bittersweet
   chocolate chips

1 (13.5oz/400ml) can full fat
   coconut milk

½ cup (120g) nut butter

2 tbsp unsweetened cocoa
   powder

3 tbsp maple or agave syrup

¾ tsp ground cinnamon

½ tsp ground ginger

¼ tsp ground black pepper

¼ tsp ground cloves

¼ tsp ground cardamom

1 tsp vanilla extract

pinch of salt

The easiest vegan ice cream there is! All you need is a freezer, nut butter, and a can of coconut milk. The coconut flavor is very subtle, the star of the show being the cocoa and all the lovely chai spices.

1 Melt the chocolate chips*.

2 In a large blender, add the melted chocolate chips and all remaining ingredients. Blend until smooth.

3 Transfer to a freezer-safe container and freeze for 4 hours. Serve immediately after the 4 hours are up. If frozen any longer, let thaw for 20 minutes before serving. This can be stored in the freezer for up to two weeks.

Note:

*Place the chocolate in a microwave-safe bowl. Microwave for 30 seconds at a time, removing and stirring between, until the chocolate has melted thoroughly.

INDEX